The Magic of Precious Stones

A modern *lapidarium* that reveals the religious, magical and symbolic uses of precious stones, their links with astrology and their mysterious healing properties.

By the same author
METAL MAGIC
THE PSYCHIC GARDEN

The Magic of Precious Stones

by

Mellie Uyldert

Translated from the Dutch by Transcript

TURNSTONE PRESS LIMITED
Wellingborough, Northamptonshire

First published in Holland as
Verborgen krachten der edelstenen
© De Driehoek, Amsterdam
First English edition published 1981
Second Impression 1983
Third Impression 1984
Fourth Impression 1985
Fifth Impression 1986

British Library Cataloguing in Publication Data

Uyldert, Mellie
　　The magic of precious stones
　　1. Occult sciences
　　2. Gems
　　I. Title　　II. Verborgen krachten der
edelstenen. *English*
　　153　　　BF1442.G/
ISBN 0-85500-138-0

*Turnstone Press is part of the
Thorsons Publishing Group*

Printed and bound in Great Britain

CONTENTS

INTRODUCTION

In writing this book on precious stones and their powers I have put together everything I thought might interest and benefit readers. Before dealing with the individual stones, I should like to mention some general considerations.

Anyone reading the book straight through will notice that some things already mentioned in the preliminary chapters are repeated in the sections on the various stones. This repetition is deliberate and has been done to make it easier to locate information on specific stones.

Some will peruse this modern lapidarium out of curiosity, others will want to put it to good use. It seems to me that those who are not content to follow old recipes or the experience of others but want to *understand* what they are doing, will find in *astrology* the one true basis of all forms of natural healing, whether they use the four elements or herbs or stones. An insight into cosmic relationships, laws and rhythms gives man the wisdom that makes him independent of teaching, tradition and experiment. I hope this book will help the reader gain such an insight.

1.

THE ORIGIN OF PRECIOUS STONES

As Above, So Below

In order to trace the origin of precious stones, we have to go far back to the genesis of our planet Earth. In addition to the approach through scientific research, which is carried out by causal thinking, there is another type of approach which uses analogical thinking. We see that a single scheme is followed in the creation of each form of life on earth and so, by analogy, we can make the assumption that something similar took place in primeval times.

The Development of Man

The development of man from conception to death proceeds according to one and the same plan. In this we see, as it were, that the nine months of formation in the womb are the prehistory of a man. At conception his etheric pattern was already determined, but it had still to gradually assume the density of a material body. This is where the great cosmic forces that some refer to as the planetary spirits or archangels come in. Each month one of these powers builds those organs in the developing body that are most in agreement with his own essential nature. How the mutual relationships of these powers works out depends on their aspects with one another at the moment of conception, and that happens just as the pattern dictates. This pattern already enshrines the persistent ego and is connected with previous manifestations of that ego.

The sacred process of development of the life-form takes place within the protecting enclosure of the uterus and of the bag of waters, corresponding to the egg-shell of the bird. The growing embryo floats in the amniotic fluid, and is nourished by its mother's blood through the umbilical cord.

In order to separate the embryo from its surroundings and, at the same time, in order to enable it to interact with these surroundings, the force that we call Saturn forms around the body the skin with its hair and nails and within the body it forms the skeleton and teeth. These solid and hard parts of the body are the most dense and although they are constantly being renewed, they present themselves to us as the final phase of the process of condensation and compaction into thick matter.

The Development of the Earth

The development of the earth can be seen as paralleling that of man; his development being always a repetition of that of the Earth on which he lives. In its prehistoric or embryonic period, its present body was only in the process of formation. Its pattern was materializing through the action of cosmic forces as described in Genesis. Initially, the water and the solid matter were not separated from one another. The basic substance of the earth floated around like a slimy mass or yolk. So, too, the embryo of man is suspended in jelly and is wrapped in membranes that close it in.

In the Saturn stage, the liquid was divided from the gas and the solid matter and the 'jelly' was partitioned into land, water and air. The human foetus, too, is bounded by its own skin and shape. Then, in the primeval 'soup', as in man, the representatives of planetary influences began to work on the 'jelly' by supplying points of origin there for the formation of their own typical organs. This work of formation then progressed, as it still does today in the embryo, so that these organs could be fit for interaction with the surrounding universe. The twelve cosmic forces incorporated mechanisms for twelve different manners of giving and taking and for twelve varieties of interaction. The same thing happens, by analogy, in the human soul and body. In man, these powers with their material instruments are called the sense organs, and in our Earth they are the precious stones. There is thus an underlying similarity between the sense-organs and the precious stones.

In addition to our six sense organs we have six more in potential. These supply the so-called clairvoyant faculties. Thus, sight has as its counterpart clairvoyance (or clear-seeing); hearing is partnered by clairaudience, etc. The ordinary sense organs are shaped by the so-called ordinary planets and the 'clairvoyant' ones by the so-called mystery planets. The work is by no means complete in regard to these; it had lapsed but is now being resumed.

Therefore, there are stones that see and stones that hear; they are the Earth's sense organs. And, on the basis of affinity, the stone that hears for the Earth can also strengthen human hearing. This is the real reason for the healing power of precious stones.

Quite apart from the sense organs, there are also other organs and faculties in man which have their analogy with precious stones; indeed, there is a connection between all stones and various parts of the body.

Anyone who knows about the existences of the twelve cosmic forces will be able to recognize their operation in the Earth, in man and in all the intermediate kingdoms of nature. Their lore is found in the so-called *doctrine of signatures,* which once guided so much of human thought. In the West this heritage from antiquity was still being enjoyed in the Middle Ages.

According to Anthroposophy, the following analogies exist between precious stones and human faculties:

chrysolite — eyesight	*beryl* — intellect
onyx — hearing, inspiration	*garnet* — imagination
carnelian — the sense of touch	*ruby* — intuition
topaz — the sense of taste	*jacinth* — spiritual sight
jasper — the sense of smell	*amethyst* — charity
emerald — the sense of motion	

Time and Place

In the preceding densification of matter, the primitive stones of the Earth developed like the human frame or skeleton, the Earth's crust grew like human nails, and the vegetation and trees sprouted like hair. Water channelled through the beds of rivers is like the various fluids flowing in the hollow vessels of our bodies, for instance in the blood vessels; the loads of ore are similar to nerves, and the gems themselves are like sense organs.

These processes of compaction and differentiation happened in parallel with one another in the age of the continent of *Lemuria,* that last remnant of the enormous earth-mass known as *Mu*. The latter once occupied the place now covered by the Pacific Ocean. It was the motherland of humanity and of civilization. The translucent suggestion of human form floated in the amniotic fluid of the earth-embryo together with translucent seaweeds, rather like the present-day lightly stained jelly-fish trailing through the ocean. Blue-green algae and the primitive ancestors of our seaweeds, mosses and ferns, consisted of very fine vessels; they formed in the jelly and dissolved again—like passing clouds.*

Silicic Acid

Gradually, the light external to the Earth forced its way into the surrounding jelly-like substance as the power of silicic acid, silica, by the action of Jupiter. This silicic acid is the great creator of precious stones. Nearly all of them consist of silicic acid and owe to it their transparency of translucency—in a word, their crystal clearness and luminosity. The various planetary powers, each of which has exhibited its individual colour in the jelly, now allowed the latter to set hard and even imparted to it patterns suggestive of vegetable fibres. Moss agate, with its patternings of tree-like and moss-like forms, is a beautiful example of this.

It is not actual plants but their patterns that are thus embedded in certain substances. It is rather striking that magnesium, the element that is an essential constituent of chlorophyll (which makes use of sunlight in every green plant), is present here. Plant patterns are etheric, but tend to condense in matter just as, to take one example, the frostwork on the window pane is made from water frozen out of the air.

The substances of which these inclusions consist, such as hornblende-asbestos, chlorite, seladonite, are compounds of silicic acid with iron, potassium, magnesium and pipe-clay. Asbestos (magnesium silicate) has plant-like vessels and can be split into thin plates. In the stones known as heliotrope (or bloodstone) and plasma, the green veins of asbestos prevent the passage of light. In other words,

---

*Since the authoress has earlier appealed to the book of Genesis, it should perhaps be pointed out that in the above poetic speculation she no longer falls into line with Genesis, which describes a clear-cut, stage-by-stage creation, in which man was made from the Earth rather than from the primeval ocean.

Translator's note.

these stones are opaque. Moss agate is really chalcedony, a translucent milky-white mineral with other materials embedded in it. The chalcedony has the maternal, nourishing character of the white albumen in an egg. It is hardly surprising that it has been used in the past as a *pietro latte* or 'milk stone' for the purpose of inducing lactation. The chrysoprase is an apple-green variety of chalcedony which owes its colour to nickel silicate and, what is more, has a fine-veined structure reminiscent of wood. Is it any wonder that the ancient Chinese regarded wood as one of the elements?

Just as a tree adds new rings of tissue each year, so a precious gem slowly adds one fine layer upon another. Agate, for example, appears to consist of alternate layers of veined chalcedony and colloidal watery opal, as many as 6000 layers being contained within the space of 1cm. The opal itself has such a watery character that it will dry out when conditions are not humid enough and will then lose its brilliance and perish. It has not travelled so far along the road to hardness as most other stones. It is possible to see in the agate how the once liquid silicic acid found openings into hollow spaces which it then proceeded to fill. Included among those precious stones that contain asbestos are the cat's eye, tiger's eye and hawk's eye, in which the fine strands of asbestos are interwoven with minute veins of quartz, the result being a beautiful silky sheen.

It is silica power that allows the fossilization of organic plant forms. Another clear example of this is chrysotile. In Arizona in North America there are petrified forests where the still upright trunks are standing like solid stones. These tree-trunks are so strong that they can be sawn through and turned into table tops with a marvellous grained effect (the area is now protected). The trees in question were related to the South American Araucaria.

Cavities and Crystals
A little reflection will show us, therefore, that we live on Earth surrounded by the petrified lives of the days of long ago; the whole of history lies around us written in stones that we use in all their stages: the peat for turf, the lignite and pit-coal as fuel, graphite for our pencils, diamonds for ornament and for drilling, and Permian natural gas and Triassic petroleum for burning. In other words we are utilizing the legacy left to us by our predecessors.

Part of this legacy are the *precious* stones, consisting of materials which have been ennobled by light until they are able to let it glow through them. In the same way there are people we instinctively recognize as noble, because the light of the spirit shines out from their eyes. The soul becomes noble when it allows the spirit's light to flow out through it. It is then in a state of illumination. The spiritual light is captured in flint, solidifying in the form of rock-crystal for example, and encounters matter in the form of lime, in which Saturn the opposite number of Jupiter finds expression. Flint is radiant and giving, whereas lime is absorbent and taking. Spirit and matter work together like these two in each living thing. Matter awaits spirit and Earth attends the coming of Heaven.

So *matter* is nothing more than what has been *formerly densified*, so that there is only a gradual increase in density between matter and spirit and thus a gradual difference in age. The older a thing is, the more hardened it is and the less active it is. Saturn is just an older brother of Jupiter.* In man, too, spirit and matter form no essential contrast, even though unintegrated people would gladly have it so. They are no more than the top and bottom layers of our human nature.

The oldest rocks in the Earth's crust, such as granite, gneiss, slate and porphyry, serve as a hard base. When these rocks were still soft, pockets of gas formed inside them, and the cavities containing the gas remained when the igneous rock solidified. There is an analogy here with the development of the human body; the embryonic blastula folds in on itself to give an inside and an outside and the inside represents, among other things, the digestive tract from mouth to anus. The womb, too, arises through an infolding process due to the astringent power of Saturn. Equally, the cavities in our primitive rocks are the wombs for much younger crystals.

The process of crystallization, both in the Earth's crust and in the human soul, is a separation of the substantial form out of the insubstantial, of the heavenly from out of the *prima materia*. This, of course, is pure alchemy. The powers of the heavenly bodies suck up towards themselves, so to speak, the substances which have an affinity with them out of the coarse mixture, and so crystals appear in the primeval rocks or even in younger layers. This is why the points of the crystals are turned upwards, away from the earth—star force is 'tugging' at them. Where there are geodes, that is to say cavities in

---

*In mythology, Jupiter (Zeus) was the son of Saturn (Chronos).

Translator's Note

which crystals are free to grow inwards, they may do so at varying angles due to the restrictions imposed on them by neighbouring crystals; however, this varying angle of growth in such circumstances does not essentially detract from the upward pulling power.

Some crystals remain below deep in the mother rock; just as many people never break free from their mothers, their families, their nation or race or their native land. They are like those who, although filled with a heavenly light of consciousness, decide to carry out their earthly task to the end. Amethysts are an example of such crystals. Other gems, such as the rock-crystal, occur with a hexagonal pyramid at each end or with some other perfect form, and have become detached from the matrix rock. These are like the individuals who travel through life with their faces towards heaven. Rock-crystal, for example, is found not only in old rocks but also in limestone, gypsum and marble, which contain liquid silicic acid even while still soft. Because they are floating in the jelly-like matrix the crystals are able to assume a double formation. Carrara marble from Italy contains multitudes of very small, very pure rock-crystals. If the marble is dissolved in hydrochloric acid, the crystals are released to become what are known as Carrara tears. Similar formations are found at Kalabagh in India and at Lake George in New York, in calcareous sandstone.

Finally, many crystals are distortions of originally different forms, as if some stronger cosmic force had overcome the first. Such processes are reminiscent of character formation in man, who builds on his inherited traits. Living is not simply doing the same thing repeatedly: it brings about changes in life-forms. In Brazil there are so-called ghost quartzes inside which there are suspended two to six smaller crystals with their surfaces all parallel to the outside surface and faintly visible. They lie in a hollow filled with gas or liquid. Like a series of Chinese boxes, each crystal lies inside the next larger and the whole thing demonstrates how the crystal grows.

It must not be thought that the cosmic forces work only on the essential parts of matter. They do more than release these; they act evenly everywhere and impress their patterns and powers on all matter as a cosmic idea. They compel matter to become the carrier and tool of their being. Sulphur, for instance is sol-fer, i.e. the Sun-bearer, and imparts the life-force of the Sun to the Earth's crust just as it does to the yolk of an egg. The cosmic forces make a home on earth for themselves, so to speak, in their own likeness. For instance, the number six as two times three is a heavenly message which can read in the tulip, the snowdrop, the lily and those flowers in general that spring from bulbs and need little soil, in the snow-flake, the cell of the honeycomb and in the rock-crystal. A different message is conveyed by the octahedral crystals of the spinel ruby or of fluorite with their triangular patterns. Then again there is the cubic crystal of rock salt (halite).

It is as if the star powers were making eyes for themselves on earth, with especially clear lenses (the precious stones) so that they could keep us under observation. The heavenly powers have not abandoned us to our fate—*they are here among us.*

2.

MAN HAS EVERYTHING
IN HIMSELF

Man is a complex being. Of high descent, he has been made a little lower than the angels and has entered this earthly plane to suffer all human ills and enjoy all human delight. He is subject to the force of the great animal instincts and his vegetative processes ally him to the plant kingdom. Finally, within a period of nine months, man's body is built up from matter (*prima materia*), the original material of creation. In his blood are to be found all the substances contained in seawater, that 'amniotic fluid' where life began to swarm. And it is just there, in matter held in shape by life, that we meet with spirit. This is depicted by the world snake surrounding the Earth's sphere and biting its own tail. The end re-enters the beginning. For as soon as centrifugal force has exhausted its influence, the centripetal force is found acting in the opposite direction; nothing in us is totally lost. Matter contains spirit. Sparks of fire are struck from the hardest substances. Matter imprisons stars of light and sparks may be struck from flints, in which they have lain asleep. But then, again, in the very dull and unattractive lumps of rock, beautiful crystals lie like a babe in the womb yet unseen until that rock is broken open to reveal them. Their formation there is a secret and sacred process. Purple amethysts grow inside grey geodes in their mother rock. They are topped by four-sided pyramids. The pointed triangles belong to the light. Even within the darkness of the mother rock the power of light arose. As soon as the rock is broken and the crystals meet the light itself, they begin to sparkle. In the same way, the eyes of newborn infants that have been formed in the dark and have never known the light, respond to the latter as soon as they encounter it. Light is already present in darkness.

How is it possible for people to think that there is no life in stones? Certainly their life is slow, but it is analogous to the life of plants and animals and men. They have a life of growth and development in form in which the same patterns are brought into being that we recognize in other kingdoms; a life in which we can detect all the vibrations which are found in the life of the human soul. The fact of the matter is that our earth has a single system of colours and a single system of numbers in which she reveals her laws at different levels and in different kingdoms of nature but always in a recognizably analogous manner.

I am gladdened by the amethyst which lies in front of me now simply because its vibrations are also running through my own soul and body. Since like answers to like, I perceive the stone with my inner eye. In the same way that nothing human is alien to me, so there is no stone on earth to which I do not respond. They speak to me and I understand their language. When a sacred stillness pervades me and my soul becomes a cathedral, where the light of the spirit shines within, then my inner amethysts flash in the mysterious depths of my being and I become aware that purple is the colour of that spiritual light that heals.

Precious stones are the eyes of matter looking at us. And many of us can hardly resist the fascination of their glance.

3.

PRECIOUS STONES AND THE SPIRITUAL LIFE

Meditation, Concentration, Inspiration, Intuition

Precious stones can be a great help in the spiritual life. Hence, they have often been used in the decoration of altars. Their beams are so pure, so direct. They are the messengers of God in a true but abstract sense and express various facets of spiritual being within the rigorous form of their crystals. While their level of material existence is characterized by their weight, hardness and chemical composition, and their level of psychic existence by their colour, their spiritual inner being is revealed by the shape and mathematical relationships of their crystals.

The best way of performing meditation with precious stones is to take one of the actual gems and to retire with it to a small consecrated room where one can be alone—an attic, for instance, high above the stir and bustle of the everyday world. Here there may be a window in the roof looking up to the clouds, the birds and the stars. The gems should be placed on velvet and kept clean.

For the purposes of meditation, a single crystal or a collection of crystals are set out and, if artificial lighting is necessary, as may be so in the evening, only candles should be used—candles made of beeswax for preference.

Take, for example, a piece of rock-crystal, a frozen moment from the effervescent life of some mountain stream; place it before you and let it speak to you evening by evening or, however often you do it, with equally spaced intervals in between. You will look forward with increasing eagerness to the times of revelation. Its six surfaces (two times three) are reminiscent of a lily or tulip. They meet in a point and thus represent the drawing together of the six of earth into the one of the spirit. There are three Yin and three Yang, for if they were all the same they would not be able to make an angle with one another. Elongated crystals tell of the indomitable striving towards the spirit imparted by silicic acid.

Or take a crystal of garnet with twelve or twenty-four faces: pyrope, almandine, spessartite. At rest in itself, it is aloof and an image of perfection. The restfulness emanating from it enables the gazer to come to himself as in the inviolable self-containment of magnesium.

Fluorite has a double four-sided pyramid, an octahedral fragment. It is much more earthly, but let it act on you.

Meditation
The stones which have traditionally been considered as most suitable for meditation are the amethyst, tourmaline or turquoise.

Concentration
The onyx is best for concentration.

Inspiration
The onyx is also used for inspiration and so, more intensely, is the aquamarine.

Intuition
The ruby is recommended for intuition. The turquoise also helps here.

Stones on the Altar
What is the purpose of an altar?

A temple or church represents the human body, the temple of the soul, the altar of which is the heart. The human heart is the dwelling of the divine spark in man and so a precious stone in an altar is there to attract the divine power out of the cosmos. The spark within the heart makes it a seat of truth, courage and love. Therefore, the altar gem must attract truth, courage and love. This is the white life-force which expresses itself in various colours; it is the divine power of the creator of the universe, expressing itself in the powers of His helpers the planetary spirits. There is one force but different forms of expression which manifest themselves according to the surface on which it is projected. In the emotions it becomes love, in the thoughts it becomes truth, in the will it becomes courage and in the body it becomes life-force.

The diamond or rock-crystal can serve as the uncoloured gem, and six further gems, this time coloured ones, can be arranged around it. Then not only does the clear white light go straight to the spark in every heart of those worshipping at the altar, but people of every type of humanity draw from the light of the stones that correspond to their type. The uncoloured light travels from spirit to spirit and the coloured light goes from soul to soul.

Everything that happens on the altar takes place in the hearts of men and women. By thinking in analogies we can see how these processes run parallel to one another.

The theosophically inclined Free Catholic Church calls the powers of the planetary spirits the Seven Rays, among which, however, they count that of the Sun. The stones are disposed by colour around the one colourless stone and form a circle in the hollow of the altar stone.

The precious stones on the altar of the Free Catholic Church are now given, with alternatives:

1. Rock-crystal
2. Lapis lazuli, turquoise, sodalite
3. Aquamarine, jade, malachite
4. Chacedony, agate, serpentine
5. Citrine, soap-stone
6. Tourmaline, garnet, carnelian, carbuncle (= dark red almandine)
7. Thulite, rhodonite

The same seven stones are set in the staff of the Free Catholic bishop and also in his pectoral cross.

Since all the elements must be represented on the altar, the stones are set out in token of the element Earth, incense is burnt to represent the element Air, the lighted candles stand for Fire and the fresh flowers speak of Water.

Similarly we have the main functions of the soul in the heart:

will and work	—	earth	—	stones
thought	—	air	—	incense
intuition, fancy	—	fire	—	candlelight
emotion	—	water	—	fresh flowers

The particular stones and flowers selected will depend on the type of person who is setting up an altar for his or her own use. Where the altar is intended for a household, provision must be made for people of every type.

An altar of this character attracts the cosmic forces automatically and radiates them out into the environment. Just as the heart propels the forces which have been taken in with the breath until they have been dispersed through the whole body, so the altar works on the fellowship of those who are worshipping or meditating.

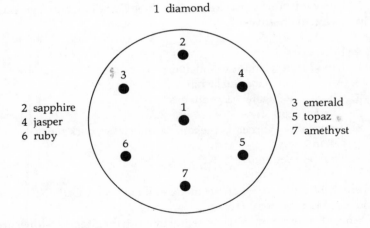

1 diamond

2 sapphire
4 jasper
6 ruby

3 emerald
5 topaz
7 amethyst

The stones on the altar of the Free Catholic Church.

4.
PRECIOUS STONES IN THE INNER LIFE

For and Against

All stones have their analogy with some part of the human soul. Three layers can be distinguished in the human soul: thinking, feeling and willing. Thinking is closest to spirit and willing is closest to body, so giving us the following analogies.

Thinking is most like the completely clear, transparent or practically transparent stones such as rock-crystal, diamond, aquamarine, emerald, and to a lesser extent ruby, topaz and sapphire.

Feeling accords with stones which are translucent, rather than transparent stones such as rose quartz, chalcedony etc., and with iridescent gems such as cat's eye and tiger's eye.

Willing is represented by compact, opaque stones like agate, turquoise, lapis lazuli, nephrite and jasper.

It is not difficult to see why the completely transparent stones were formerly the most highly prized for jewellery: in olden days it was the thinking pole of the human axis which was most highly regarded, together with the light of the spirit and a clear understanding. Nowadays, the opaque, semi-precious stones are favoured because interest is predominantly centred in earthly life.

To strengthen one or other of these functions, the appropriate stone may be worn or placed near you so that it can be concentrated on from time to time. However, each of us must choose the stone to which he or she feels drawn at a given moment.

For general use some of the indications are listed below.

For sharpening the natural or clairvoyant senses:

touch	— carnelian
hearing	— onyx, amber
sight	— emerald, beryl, amethyst (colour blindness), aquamarine, obsidian, chrysolite, malachite
smell	— jasper
taste	— topaz

For:

making the mind keener	— beryl, emerald
vitality	— agate, brown aventurine
eloquence	— agate, emerald, citrine
will-power	— beryl
memory	— emerald

Against:

misfortune	— tourmaline, carnelian, onyx, amethyst, opal
restlessness and insomnia	— stroke the forehead and temples with amethyst, topaz, jacinth, padparadschah sapphire, rhodonite
states of hypnosis, enslavement, possession	— chalcedony
low spirits, depression	— chalcedony, lapis lazuli, garnet
home-sicknesses	— amethyst, rock-crystal
inebriation	— amethyst
pain	— ruby, sardonyx
headache	— stroke the temples with magnetite

For:

protection on a journey	— emerald, tourmaline (against falls)
sailors	— aquamarine
finding a treasure .	— agate
soldiers on active service	— smoky quartz

Binding and Breaking Stones

The great binder in life and love is the blue sapphire (Taurus). It bestows fidelity and attachment when given as a love-token to a sweetheart. If someone else takes and wears it they will be bound to the original giver.

Rose quartz gives a younger and warmer love that is not quite so lasting (Venus-Moon).

The ruby gives a glowing love (Aries).

The dark-red garnet gives a more hidden love which is not exuberant but, nevertheless, deeply passionate. However, it can lead to hate and separation due to its potential jealousy (Scorpio).

On the other hand, the flesh-pink carnelian gives and strengthens the solidarity due to blood relationship, love of one's own family and an appreciation of the meaning of kinship; it encourages love between parents and children (Virgo).

The amethyst encourages the love and worship of God.

The turquoise enters into the spontaneous upsurge of romantic love and leads to remarkable encounters with people from a past life (Uranus).

Chalcedony is a binder on the mental plane for assisting connected thinking at an impersonal level. It helps in the spinning of a coherent pattern of thoughts.

5.

PRECIOUS STONES IN ASTROLOGY AND IN MAGIC

Since astrology co-ordinates and underpins all the spiritual sciences, it should always be our point of departure when we are thinking in analogies. In getting to know the essential properties of gems we can start by studying their crystalline forms, their colours, their effects on human beings and so on, but whatever we discover by these means will always fall in line with what we know of the cosmic forces.

The Planets

At least twelve planets revolve round the Sun. Man today is responding to ten of these: Mercury, Venus, Earth, Mars, Lucifer (now broken into the fragments known as the Asteroids), Jupiter, Saturn, Uranus, Neptune and Pluto. An eleventh, recently born from the Sun, has not yet been named by us. Several astrologers have speculated on the existence of planets further out then Pluto from the Sun and one of these was thought to have been discovered not very long ago.

The following arrangement is based on the colours of the precious stones and of the planetary forces:

Mercury — *yellow*: citrine, topaz, yellow sapphire
Venus   — *pink, blue*: rose quartz, blue sapphire, nephrite, emerald
Earth   — *green, light green*: aventurine, peridot (olivine, chrysolite) green jade
Mars   — *bright red*: ruby, garnet, jasper (silex)

Lucifer — *mother-of-pearl*: opal, moonstone
Jupiter — *orange, gold*: jacinth, topaz, orange carnelian
Saturn — *dark green, black*: onyx, jet, spinel ruby
Uranus — *blue-green*: turquoise, malachite, amazonite
Neptune — *lilac, violet*: amethyst, opal
Pluto — *dark red*: bloodstone, dark red agate (pyrope),
almandine

The correspondences for the 'Lights' are:

Sun — diamond, rock crystal
Moon — moonstone, chalcedony, rhinestone, opal

The Signs of the Zodiac

The consonance of the Signs of the Zodiac with given gems depends mainly on the effects of the stones produced by the forces dwelling within them. It is no more than a half-truth to say that people ought to wear their birth stones in accordance with that Sign of the Zodiac occupied by the Sun when they were born. The stone will certainly fortify the individual's vitality and will, because the Sun represents these, but if there are difficult aspects to the Sun made by one or more planets in the horoscope such inherent conflicts will also be strengthened and activated. The upshot will be increased problems and tasks which, if bravely faced, will bring maturity, but not otherwise. Generally speaking, it is wise to wear the particular stone which will lend support to any factor in the horoscope that is rather too weak, should it be thought desirable to do so.

Month stones are pieces of nonsense. The Sun changes sign between the 19th and 24th of each month and each month is different. Some stones suit several Signs because they harbour a number of different powers.

Before making a choice, read through the description of each stone in turn.

As a rule, the inner relationship between certain gems and the Signs of the Zodiac is as follows:

Aries (Ram) — jasper, ruby
Taurus (Bull) — blue sapphire, rose quartz, lapis
lazuli

Gemini (Twins)	— citrine, rock-crystal, aquamarine, cat's eye, tiger's eye
Cancer (Crab)	— emerald, olivine, serpentine (white), chalcedony
Leo (Lion)	— gold quartz, almandine (carbuncle), olivine (chrysolite), diamond
Virgo (Virgin)	— carnelian, agate, sardonyx
Libra (Scales)	— emerald, aventurine, padparadschah sapphire, jade, nephrite
Scorpio (Scorpion)	— garnet, bloodstone (haematite), beryl, pyrope, spinel ruby
Sagittarius (Archer)	— topaz, jacinth
Capricorn (Sea-goat)	— smoky quartz, onyx, jet
Aquarius (Water-bearer)	— turquoise, malachite, amazonite
Pisces (Fishes)	— amethyst, opal, moonstone, rhinestone

The choice of a gemstone to wear will depend in the first place on personal taste and intuition. There will be an inner feeling as to what is the suitable stone at the moment of choice.

Charging Stones

In order to give a stone still more power than it has already, it may be charged with extra force. If, for example, a Scorpio stone is being given to someone whose Sun Sign is Scorpio to make him stronger, it is best to charge this stone when the Sun and Moon are both in Scorpio as shown in the ephemeris (the astrological almanac) and especially between midnight and noon if possible. The stone is laid, if it is a new one, on the private altar. If it once belonged to someone else, it must be first neutralized by laying it for twenty-four hours in running water, by passing it through a flame three times, by burying it in the earth for a little while or by hanging it in the smoke of incense for a time— whichever is preferred.

The precious stone is placed on linen or pure silk on the private altar, surrounded by living flowers, burning incense (genuine olibanum, grains of resin on glowing charcoal) and three lighted wax candles. With the right hand (or with the left hand if the individual is left-handed) a well-closed circle is described around the altar. The hands are then laid one on top of the other, palms downward, with the bestowing hand on top (e.g. the right hand in right-handed persons) and the wish, prayer or dedication is then sung in order to bring the chosen power into the stone for the benefit of the intended wearer. Each wish must be repeated three times in exactly the same words, for messages presented to angels are merely noticed the first time, are given serious consideration the second time, and the third time are productive of positive results. To close, the word *a-u-m* is uttered and the protective circle is 'redrawn'. The candles are left burning a little longer. Once it has been charged, the stone is put in a small box and given as soon as possible to the person for whom it is intended.

It goes without saying that for best results the operator must be pure without and within. He or she should be sober and well rested and be fresh from a bath or a good wash, and fresh air should have been deeply breathed into the lungs seven times. The clothing should be clean and not made of plastic or synthetic fibres but preferably of linen or natural silk, and the feet should be bare but clean. One window must be open and the operator must stand facing the sun.

Talismans and Amulets

People have been engaged in making talismans, amulets and mascots from ancient times in the hope that these would give protection, health and help. These articles can be either representational or symbolic. Examples of representational objects are the little dolls or toy animals hanging in cars. These serve as a projection: a partner which is the double of the self. In a sense they are idols, to the extent that the doll is thought to be indwelt by the higher self. If bad luck threatens the self, the higher self will now take that bad luck on himself or herself. It is just like the totem animal that is thought to guard the well-being of a tribe. The animal contains the cosmic power enabling it to meet the needs of every member of its tribe. As long as a person has not realized himself or herself as an individual, that person's connection with the life source has to be preserved intact.

But as soon as the individual is there, standing on his own two feet, as soon as he *is* someone, he has no further need for mascots. He then has his own personal relationship with his fate and his higher self is felt within him, not seen as an outside projection.

Symbolic objects are completely different. A symbolic object is a regular figure, a pattern borrowed from creation. Examples are a circle, a circle with a central point, an ordinary cross, a fylfot, a triangle, a square, a pentagon, a pentagram, a hexagon and a hexagram, etc. These are the basic designs man observes in nature before he starts to make things for himself; they occur in flowers and shells, in leaves and snowflakes, in the house of the snail and in crystals. Man has adapted them for his buildings and ornaments and for his dance figures. It was then that he made the discovery that the patterns actually *worked*, that they radiated or absorbed certain forces, that they made something happen in their surroundings. He observed that, by describing certain figures with the movements of his body, he himself could produce definite effects. In this way the sacred symbol and the sacred dance were born.

A symbol is a picture with an underlying meaning; it is a sign or a 'signature' of something; it is an expression on the material plane of a figure composed of lines of force in the invisible ether. It is an operation that has been frozen in matter yet is accompanied by supplementary etheric action. If a symbol is placed on or in a house, it will be constantly acting there and the sphere of influence in that house will become more and more adapted to the symbol. The cosmic forces attracted by the symbol will bless the house.

This is the origin of the sacred signs or runes in their 'decorative' use on houses. For instance, there is the sign of the two swans in Friesland, the horse's head in Saxony, the cross seen in French-speaking districts and the diamond-shaped rune *Ing* in traditional Scandinavian sky-lights and Odin's mark on shutters.

As above, so below; but also as below, so above. Just as a cosmic force expresses itself in a certain number or in a certain geometrical shape, so that number or shape will attract this cosmic force and will form a point of support for it; because the cosmic forces are every-where present like radio waves in the ether, and where a receiver is available, there they are trapped, transformed and used.

If a sacred symbol or a rune is carved out of wood and set on a rooftop to stand against the sky, or is painted on a door or is built into a stone wall, or is embroidered on an article of clothing or is cut into the wood of some useful object, or is drawn on paper or parchment to be worn inside a locket, it becomes a talisman. This is no joke. People have been working in an office in an unpleasant atmosphere of rivalry and dispute and, after someone has placed a favourable rune drawn on paper underneath a table-top, the atmosphere has improved.

Should great need be felt for a certain power, the large-scale symbol of that power can be painted on paper and hung beside the work-bench or bed. It will work. Many people hang a motto on the wall. This works in two ways at the same time. Firstly, by the impression made by the words themselves on our conscious minds as we keep reading them, and secondly, by the form of the letters, which are symbols in their own right that attract certain forces and create patterns in the ether. Letters are themselves sacred symbols.

Some people engrave a religious text on a precious stone, to be worn next to the skin. Here the talisman takes the form of a gem; again with a double action—the words have their own effect and the power drawn from the cosmos by the stone assists them. This is then a true talisman and anyone who understands how it works will wear it not out of superstition but out of faith mixed with knowledge.

The breastplate of the high priest.

So if a precious stone is worn that suits the personality of the wearer, if it is charged with the desired power, if it is engraved with a sacred symbol plus certain holy words, then its action is fourfold.

Astrology in its widest sense is the knowledge of the laws and rhythms of the cosmos in which we live.

Magic is the knowledge and skill to apply the laws and rhythms of the etheric plane to the plane of matter.

Astrology makes a man knowledgable and knowing.

Magic helps a man to know what he is doing and to do what he knows.

6.

PRECIOUS STONES IN RELIGION

Precious stones have been placed in temples down the ages not merely as adornments but, first and foremost, on account of their *radiations*. Were not the chief deities of most nations in antiquity the twelve planetary spirits whose vibrations were encountered in certain colours and in certain gems? So all twelve had to be represented, including the stones for the Sun and the Moon, and perhaps for a number of lesser gods. Naturally, most use would have been made of the gems that occurred locally. Therefore, it came about that the temples became extremely powerful fields of force which charged each worshipper with their energies, activating all his abilities, healing him, comforting him and renewing his self-confidence, and so disposing him to be happy and even jubilant.

The topaz, ruby and emerald mines of the Incas in ancient Mexico were fantastically productive and the temples and palaces of these people were beautifully adorned with gems. Although the Spanish conquistadors plundered the treasures, a part of the latter was safely hidden away, no one knows where. Perhaps this statement should be modified, since one place of concealment is in fact known; but whoever goes digging there always comes to grief. Today, Brazil is still the biggest source of precious and semi-precious stones.

Central Europe is another area where the mystique associated with precious stones has been preserved. This is especially true of Bohemia, that land where from time immemorial beauty and mysticism have been fused to provide a rich human delight, where glass blowing is done to satisfy a purely artistic urge and the violin maker wends his way through the Erzgebirge forests laying his ear against the trunks of trees so that he may choose for his violins wood which already vibrates with the murmur of music. It is there that the lover of precious stones will visit the cathedral of the Hradschin, the royal citadel above Prague, and enter the mortuary chapel of Vaclav or 'Good King Wenceslas', where the walls are covered with dark red pyrope-agate, which is found there in profusion, and everything gleams with gold and gems. Anyone who enters that place can feel their power and recognizes that he is in a sacred shrine.

Then again, in the neighbourhood of Prague, there is the castle, Karlstein, where the Emperor Charles IV founded a sanctuary, in one of the keeps, for a chosen band of knights who knew and served the jewel in their own hearts. There they met, and their painted portraits are still hanging on the walls of gold. Suspended from the golden arches leading into the chancel are enormous precious stones hanging on threads. In the gilded ceiling are set crystal stars, a gold sun and a silver moon. Once inside, the hidden flame of the heart leaps upward and is consumed by mystic longings.

What then is Bohemia, if not a land of music and art, of Scorpio and Taurus, of deep, dark red passion for the beauty of the spirit expressed in matter?

Nowadays, in the great Christian cathedrals of Europe, the jewel-encrusted treasures of the Church are seldom used in divine service; instead, they are often laid up in crypts where anyone who wishes to see them must first pay an entry fee—so totally has it been forgotten why jewels adorn the holy vessels. In just the same way, many folk allow the priceless assets they possess to slumber in their unconscious while they spend their lives in the drabness of dutiful toil.

The High Priest's Breastplate*
In the Bible we read of the twelve stones ordained to be set in the breast-plate of the high priest of Israel, for wearing in the services of the tabernacle and in the temple of Solomon. These stones corresponded to the twelve sons of Jacob and to the twelve tribes descended from them. Exodus 39:8 ff. says: 'And he made the breastplate . . . It was foursquare; they made the breastplate double . . . And they set in it four

---

*See the illustration on page 31.

rows of stones. The rows were of three stones each and consisted of:

red jasper	chrysolite	malachite
haematite	lapis lazuli	prase
amber	agate	amethyst
turquoise	chrysoprase	nephrite

'They were inclosed in ouches of gold (settings of gold) in their inclosings. And the stones were according to the names of the children of Israel, twelve, according to their names, like the engravings of a signet, every one with his name, according to the twelve tribes.'

Prase is a translucent, leek-green form of quartz. According to another version, the list is:

carnelian	topaz	emerald
carbuncle	sapphire	jasper
opal	agate	amethyst
chrysolite	onyx	sardonyx

English versions also differ in their renderings of the original Hebrew names of these stones.

Sardonyx is an onyx made up of multi-coloured layers.

The various translators must bear the responsibility for their very disparate renderings; we shall merely content ourselves with asking how the stones suit the twelve sons of Jacob according to the brief description of their natures.

Aries	Simeon	— ruby, red jasper (silex), Indian carnelian
Taurus	Levi	— sapphire, rose quartz
Gemini	Naphtali	— citrine, gold topaz, cat's eye, tiger's eye
Cancer	Asher	— chrysoprase, aventurine, olivine
Leo	Judah	— chrysolite, rock crystal
Virgo	Issachar	— carnelian, yellow agate
Libra	Dan	— emerald, nephrite, jade
Scorpio	Benjamin	— garnet, bloodstone, red tourmaline
Sagittarius	Reuben	— chalcedony
Capricorn	Gad	— onyx, jet
Aquarius	Joseph	— turquoise, malachite
Pisces	Zebulon	— amethyst, aquamarine

The Stones of the New Jerusalem

In the book of Revelation we find the twelve precious stones named once more, but now as the foundations of the wall of the city, New Jerusalem, and in them 'the names of the twelve apostles of the Lamb.*' According to the Dutch translation of 1957, these precious stones are named as follows:

diamond	lapis lazuli	ruby
emerald	sardonyx	sardius
topaz	beryl	chrysolite
chrysoprase	sapphire	amethyst

Hence these are not exactly the same stones as in the breastplate of the high priest.

The Leyden Version gives a completely different classification.

The crozier of a Catholic bishop, his pectoral cross, the altar stones, the candlesticks and certain crosses carry all seven stones, according to the seven rays or planets:

1. Diamond (rock crystal)
2. Sapphire (lapis lazuli, turquoise, sodalite)
3. Emerald (aquamarine, jade, malachite)
4. Jasper (chalcedony, agate, serpentine)
5. Topaz (citrine, soap-stone)
6. Ruby (tourmaline, garnet, carnelian, carbuncle)
7. Amethyst (thulite, rhodonite)

In the episcopal cross the amethyst comes in the middle with the sapphire under it, the diamond above it and amethysts again at the extremities. According to the Anglican and Free Catholic 'bishop', Leadbeater, the Theosophist and occultist, from whom this information has been taken, the diamond's place will be in the middle a thousand years hence when the next root race** has made its appearance.

The diamond is also found in the centre of an *Egyptian ankh*, where

---

*The authoress says here, 'according to the twelve tribes of Israel' and regards the stones as the foundations of the twelve city gates. However, the book of Revelation says that the stones were the foundations of the whole wall. It was the gates of pearl themselves which had the names of the twelve tribes written on them.   *Translator's note.*

the circle meets the cross; the ends of the arms of the cross were set with
a topaz on the left and with an emerald on the right; the vertical bar
carried a carnelian in the centre and a jasper at its foot and on the circle
there were five stones: an amethyst at the top, an onyx on the left with a
ruby under that and on the right an opal with a sapphire below.

Anthroposophy goes deepest of all into this subject and is very
systematic in its approach. It sees the four rows of stones in the breastplate of the high priest of Israel as corresponding to the four elements—
which is fairly obvious. Each element then takes three tribes grouped as
follows:

Fire	— Taurus (sardius)	— Gemini (sapphire)	— Cancer (amethyst)
Air	— Leo (topaz)	— Virgo (diamond)	— Libra (turquoise)
Water	— Scorpio (emerald)	— Sagittarius (lapis lazuli)	— Capricorn (onyx)
Earth	— Aquarius (ruby)	— Pisces (agate)	— Aries (jasper)

However, it should be mentioned that this attribution of the
elements is in conflict with the way they are assigned in astrology.
What is more, it does not tally with anything to be found in the Old
Testament.

The twelve foundation stones in the wall of the New Jerusalem are as
follows:

Aries	— jasper	Libra	— chrysolite
Taurus	— sapphire	Scorpio	— beryl
Gemini	— chalcedony	Sagittarius	— topaz
Cancer	— emerald	Capricorn	— chrysoprase
Leo	— sardonyx	Aquarius	— jacinth
Virgo	— sardius (carnelian)	Pisces	— amethyst

When this is explained it gives evidence of an orderly arrangement

---

**Some writers of a past generation thought this would take place in Australia
and North America, but much of what they taught was coloured by Victorian
ideas on race and evolution.   *Translator's note.*

(see Dr M. L. Stibbe: *Edelsteen en Mens*—Gems and Humanity).*

In my opinion, this is the correct correspondence between the Signs and the Stones.

The twelve disciples also take their place in the scheme:

Peter	— Aries	James son of	
Andrew	— Taurus	Alphaeus	— Sagittarius
James	— Gemini	Thaddeus	— Capricorn
John	— Cancer	Simon called	
Philip	— Leo	Zelotes	— Aquarius
Bartholomew	— Virgo	Matthias	
Matthew	— Libra	(who replaced	
Thomas	— Scorpio	Judas)	— Pisces

I am not completely in agreement here since Judas Iscariot, for instance, would definitely not have belonged to Pisces but to the Scorpio-Taurus axis, and Doubting Thomas clearly belonged to Virgo.

The exact pattern in which the stones, sign-types and Bible characters are interrelated depends on the level at which they are viewed, whether as individual entities in their own right, as symbols, as components of a greater whole or in some other manner. Each arrangement has a right to exist and one does not exclude another.

The Bible itself is true at all levels, whether literal and factual, or symbolic of the inner life of man, or symbolic of the outworking of cosmic law, or purely spiritual.

The radiations from precious stones bring into manifestation the corresponding forces in man's inner being and then activate these forces.

Christianity attached most value to the virtues of Pisces: self-sacrifice, meekness, purity and spirituality, and these are promoted by the amethyst and by purple stones in general. Hence the use of the amethyst in the bishop's ring. The diamond is set in the centre of the crozier and of the ankh, because its light is white and the colours of the surrounding stones are fractions of this light.

The cardinal's ring contains a sapphire, an obvious sign and seal of his faithfulness to the Church.

---

*See also 'A Rebirth of Images' by Austin Farrer, Dacre Press, 1949. However Dr Farrer attributes the Signs differently.   *Translator's note.*

The Pope wears a jasper in his ring; the stone of the Ram, the foundation, but wholly opaque; materialized without any light.

Stones of Various Cultures

Every 2160 years the first point of Aries moves into another Zodiacal constellation and so ushers in a new culture pattern and a civilization is formed with its characteristic styles of art, science and religion. Certain stones then come to the fore in public worship and in cultic use. Because they have been employed in ornaments and useful articles and in talismans left with the dead, and have since come to light in excavations and finds, they supply us with a picture of what was most valued at the time. The objection may be raised that such stones were simply the ones readily available, but that is not so; other, rarer stones have been found among the rest. The peoples of antiquity were not really bothered by whether a thing was easy or not—after all, they kept thousands of slaves to toil for them. Desirable gems were often fetched from far away simply because their virtues were prized.

Indian Culture and the Moonstone

Some 10,000 years ago, when the first point of Aries entered Cancer the Crab, the constellation with the same name as the sign that is ruled by the Moon,* the old Indian culture began to flower and continued until 6000 B.C. We come across what is left of it among the remains of the old temples, which were built up of terraced galleries covered in relief-work full of representations of the ancient myths and showing all the wars, loves and adventures of the gods, whose forms were spawned by an inexhaustible fantasy. The modern visitor is almost overwhelmed by the rich vividness of it all. Now this is just the domain of the Moon in mankind: she governs imagination and imagery and the colourful emotional life. No wonder the moonstone was so highly prized and so widely used during this period. The soul was then cradled in an ideal world of gods and goddesses, whose activities were shared by exuberant animals amid profusely springing vegetation. Sexual life is depicted in endless variety on the temple walls and this, too, belongs to the sphere occupied by the Moon in our lives.

---

*The original says simply '. . . Cancer the Crab, the Sign that is ruled by the Moon', but in traditional Western astrology the signs and constellations are treated as distinct.   *Translator's note.*

Persian Culture and the Turquoise

When the First Point of Aries entered Gemini the Twins, the Indian culture began to fossilize, but in ancient Persia a religion and culture appeared led by Spitama, who was a great spiritual leader, a zaradusht, zarathustra or Zoroaster. He developed the Gemini pattern into a new doctrine and way of life. The Twins typify dualism or that which is twofold, and the religion which arose under their influence emphasized the duality of Good and Evil, of Ormuzd and Ahriman; though not with a dread sense of sin and guilt, for Gemini is a light and sunny sign belonging to the element Air. Correct breathing was taught not only to the religious devotees but to every child at home as part of its education.

The ancient Persians were not surrounded by the same abundant plant-life that had supported the Indians but, guided by their teacher and their own understanding, started to improve their produce by cross-breeding and to develop the potential of the plant we know today as wheat.

Now, the turquoise is a stone with two colours—green and blue. It represents the green of the fields and the blue of devotion with which man seeks to put theory into practice in everyday life. Not dreams but deeds.

Egyptian Culture and Malachite

From 6000 to 4000 years ago the First Point of Aries moved through the Sign of Taurus the Bull. In Egypt at that time, the sacred bull Apis was worshipped. A handsome animal was chosen (by means of a small mark) and cared for in the temple as if it were indwelt by the god himself. When it was full-grown, it was conveyed in a golden barque over the Nile to the temple in Memphis. The children of Israel in the Sinai desert decided to worship a bull-god and made the *golden calf*.

The ruler of Taurus is Venus, whose metal is copper. Now malachite and azurite are two minerals with a high copper content and they are invariably found together, in the upper layers of mines. These were the favourite stones of the Egyptian culture period.

Egyptian ladies carried in their vanity-cases a small tray containing a beauty cream made of finely-ground malachite mixed into fat. With this they painted their eyelids and even the hair of their heads. The excrement of flies rubbed down on a malachite slab was used as an eye ointment for the eye disease that ravaged the land of Egypt in those days. Malachite is green and azurite is blue.

The dark blue lapis lazuli was also much used, and out of it the scarab, or sacred dung-beetle, was carved, among other things. It was worn as a talisman against disaster. All three were typical Taurus stones, in restful Yin colours, very suitable for a passive, sensual and materialistic people who were blindly reliant on their priests.

The Graeco-Roman Culture and the Agate

4000 years ago, when the First Point of Aries entered Aries the Ram, the Egyptians began to pay special honour to the Ram god Ammon. The Israelites brought offerings of rams and put the nation's sins on the scapegoat, and the frequent battles between Greek city states gave rise to a new form of culture in which athletic champions and war heroes were honoured by men with a typical Aries mentality. Sparta, which was completely given over to physical culture and the pursuit of glory, was an extreme expression of the qualities of this martial sign.

Rome conquered Greece, absorbed her culture and became the nation whose legions subjugated a large part of Europe and North Africa. It was a nation orientated to the Aries-Libra axis, making both wars and laws. It overcame other nations by force of arms (Aries) and then entered into alliances with them (Libra). When the spear in the hand of the image of Mars in the temple of that god began to shake, that was the sign for a fresh campaign and the troops marched out through the gate of Janus and onto the field of battle.

Soldiers were only too ready to wear some talisman on their persons. Such talismans were cameos made of agate and sardonyx and were engraved with the picture of the guardian spirit or with a suitable saying or symbol.

Agate belongs to what is human and personal. Roman religion concentrated entirely on externals. Strange gods were imported from foreign lands and were installed in fashionable temples without any deep feelings of devotion. However Mithraism, which was very popular, set forth the ideal of self-development and independence symbolized by the slaying of the bull, for the age of Taurus was over.

The Christian Culture and the Amethyst

And then, 2000 years ago, the First Point of Aries entered Pisces the Fishes. From the Ram to the Fishes is the biggest changeover that can take place between two divisions of the Zodiac. It was an enormous leap from the Ram culture, which was dedicated to the earthly and human, to the Fishes culture with its renunciation of all earthly things. Pisces is the Sign of the oppressed, the slaves and the martyrs, of drunkards and saints. The first in Rome to realize the new pattern were the Christian converts, who inscribed the sign of the Fish on the walls of the catacombs in which they gathered in secret to hold their services. And so the Christian Church came into prominence with its ideal image of self-sacrifice and purification from all that is egotistic. The cleansing, violet amethyst was the very stone to help in this. It sheds a pure light into the sinful soul and directs the attention to the things of the spirit. Because sexual activities were regarded as sinful, the amethyst was worn as a protector of chastity and a safeguard against

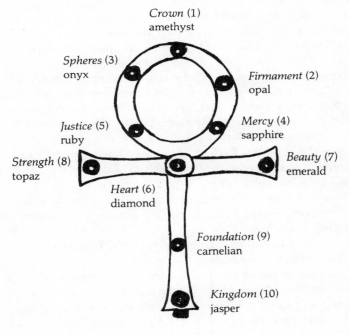

Crown (1)
amethyst

Spheres (3)
onyx

Firmament (2)
opal

Justice (5)
ruby

Mercy (4)
sapphire

Strength (8)
topaz

Beauty (7)
emerald

Heart (6)
diamond

Foundation (9)
carnelian

Kingdom (10)
jasper

The Ankh

Translator's Note: The student of the Qabalah will notice that the above pattern is based on that of the Sephirotic Tree, although (as in the misplacement of 'Beauty') does not follow that pattern exactly.

seduction. It was used for meditation and for obtaining spiritual sight. It is the stone of the priest and is preferably worn on the third finger of the left hand.

The amethyst has accompanied the Christian culture throughout the past 2000 years. In the sixteenth century is cost as much as a diamond and was just as highly prized (*before* the vast deposits of precious stones in South America had been discovered). It was an especial favourite in the Piscean country of Russia:* the Czar possessed 20 thrones for different times of year and for special occasions and, in 1660, Czar Alexis was presented with a throne which had been decorated by the Armenian Zachary Saradorow with 867 diamonds and 1223 amethysts. Another throne, known as the Persian because it was a gift from the Shah to Czar Ivan IV, was adorned with 1325 rubies and jacinths, 539 turquoises, many pearls, sapphires and peridots (olivines) and 15 especially beautiful amethysts.

The amethyst imparts spiritual power. Hence its appropriateness in the Czar's throne and in the bishop's ring.

---

*Astrologers assign post-revolutionary Russia to Aquarius, as they did pre-revolutionary Red Russia (e.g. Sibley in 1784). Anthroposophical writers seem to prefer the above. *Translator's note.*

7.

THE STONES LIVE IN US

The Magic Wand

In addition to having a spiritual spark in his heart, a soul and a physical body, man has a finer, etheric body or *subtle body*, with lines of electrical and magnetic force passing through it. Occultists have known of it for many years, clairvoyants have seen it and now science has discovered it.

The lines of force pass through 'transformers' in stages from below upwards, becoming more refined in the process and with changes in potential. At the level of the abdomen there is what may be termed *life-force*, from the chest to the root of the nose is *soul-force* and above that is *spirit-force*.

These 'transformers' parallel the endocrine glands of the physical body. In a similar way we find electrical currents associated with the nerves and magnetic ones with the blood vessels.

From time immemorial, the subtle body has been depicted as the knotty branch of a tree used as a traveller's staff. Later it became the staff of the beadle, the mayor and the parliamentary mace-bearer, also that of the magician or of the bishop. Precious stones set in some of these rods of power represent the 'transformers' and operate like them too, for a symbol is never a mere decoration. It works to bring into being the thing it symbolizes. The lower acts on the higher. Therefore in the old mystery plays the progress of the human soul was exhibited in the hope that souls would be encouraged to develop further along the appointed path. The magic wand in the hand of each Atlantean (see

The Coming Race by Bulwer Lytton) was constructed in the same manner. Man keeps on making reproductions of himself.

The planetary forces come to a focus in the 'transformers', both in our subtle bodies and in the endocrine glands of our physical bodies, and so we have a magic wand. Whoever knows how to use it can do wonders. The transformers can be fortified by the wearing of certain gems on the appropriate parts of the body. This is also how we make contact with the healing powers of gems.

The Ankh

As already mentioned, a tree trunk is often seen as analogous to the human body. Hence the veneration of some tree on solemn occasions, either where it stands or when cut down and erected as a Christmas tree or maypole for example (or, viewed symbolically the tree of knowledge and the tree of life). The human body when standing up straight with legs together and arms outspread has the shape of a tree. Here is the origin of the sacred symbol known to the ancient Egyptians as the *ankh*. The circle stands on a vertical bar and also directly above a horizontal bar crossing the latter. The circle represents the human head above a vertical trunk and legs and horizontally held arms. Assuming the circle indicates spirit and the cross indicates matter, we have here *spirit over matter*. I once came across, in a now defunct magazine, an article by S. Alphard on an Egyptian talisman of ivory in the form of an ankh which was set with ten different precious stones. It might be worth our while taking a look at this piece of craftsmanship in order to gain a better understanding of planets, men and stones; for each planet expresses itself in one particular stone, although of course the actual choice of stones could have been different. Local stones are used as far as possible. (A talisman is an object that is supposed to attract the good powers, unlike an amulet, which serves to ward off the evil powers.)

A glance at the sketch of this ankh will show that there is a diamond at the point where the circle meets the top centre of the 'T'—the place of the heart! Halfway down the vertical bar there is a carnelian and at its base there is a jasper. There is a topaz on the left-hand end of the horizontal bar and on the right-hand end an emerald. The circle contains five stones. There is an amethyst at the very top; under this on the left is an onyx and on the right an opal. Lastly, we have a ruby on the left nearer the bottom of the circle and on the right a sapphire. If we now consider this ankh as being like a tree or rather a man, with the stones as 'transformers' and endocrine glands with correspondences to certain planets, we can analyze it as follows:

Jasper. This is a stone of Pluto, the god of the underworld, and here indeed he is found at the foot of man, the root of the tree. Pluto is also the magician, and jasper is reputed to protect against witchcraft. In Christian symbology, however, it speaks of the power of the Holy Spirit, the Creator Spiritus, and the light of the New Jerusalem is described, in the book of Revelation, as 'like a jasper stone, clear as crystal'—transparent therefore, although the stone we call jasper is opaque and white, grey, yellow or reddish brown in colour or sometimes golden. The power that lies within it has not yet manifested itself, but is at the point where it is about to descend into matter (Anthroposophy calls jasper the stone of Aries: the incarnation).

The power of the Earth enters the human body at the feet and here is the first 'transformer', where the Earth's energy is changed into human energy.

Carnelian. The next 'transformer' on the way up is associated with the sex organs, which serve for reproduction and divide the life force into male and female. It is ruled by the Moon, which governs family and racial unity and strengthens blood ties and love between parents and children. These are also the properties of this virginal stone, which occurs in pink, terracotta, liver or flesh colours.

Diamond. In the centre of the ankh, the Sun is couched in the heart and solar plexus, and this is the proper place for the colourless and luminous diamond. There the power of truth, love and courage is diffused to all sides like sunlight. Here lies the thymus gland.

Topaz. The topaz, the stone of Mercury, lies on the right of ankh as we look at it. This is the side of thinking and respiration and here the primitive energy is transformed into thought-power and consciousness.

Emerald. On the left is the green emerald, which is associated with the emotions. It is the stone of Venus, the Esmeralda of the Aztecs. It strengthens the throat centre, which converts cosmic energy into creative word and song. The thyroid gland is involved too.

Sapphire. In the circle representing the head and the inner life, we find the blue sapphire (sapphires also occur in other colours) as the stone of Jupiter, of religious devotion, and of inner devotion and faith. However, in an engagement ring, this stone also belongs to Venus.

Ruby. Opposite the sapphire stands the red ruby of Mars, the stone of passion. It belongs to the ear and nose area (corresponding to the male genitals).

Onyx. Above the last stone is the shining black onyx of Saturn, which belongs to the thought centre behind the forehead. The onyx is able to improve objective thinking and also fends off undesirable influences such as the 'evil eye'.

Opal. The contrasting white opal represents the opposite pole to the onyx on the ankh. Because it has a many-coloured iridescent sheen, we can see the influence of Uranus in it. Uranus is linked with the pituitary gland or hypophysis in the head, which among other things makes it possible for a person to interact with the environment. In my opinion, the turquoise would have been even better than the opal in this position.

Amethyst. Shining at the top is the stone of Neptune, the purple amethyst, the stone of soul cleansing and spiritual ennoblement (the spiritual man is said to have a purple aura). It is appropriate to the pineal gland or epiphysis in the head, the seat of all knowledge, where the awareness of within and without, of one's own body, soul and spirit meet together. It is situated beneath the crown, where the heavenly light comes in and goes out and from where the soul departs on the death of the spiritually-developed individual. This is the point of excarnation, exactly opposite that of incarnation at the foot of the ankh. 'The Lord shall preserve thy going out and thy coming in from this time forth, and even for evermore'.

Two triangles are visible within the circle of the ankh. The one with its points upwards connects the amethyst, ruby and sapphire and makes the fighter for the faith (this is the Sagittarius emblem with the point upwards).

The second triangle, with the point downwards, links the onyx, opal and diamond. It teaches us that Saturnian convention and settled order (the establishment) and the Uranian revolution and renewal (inspiration, communication) are synthesized in the heart that knows the eternal truth.

Together, the two triangles compose the Star of David, the symbol of the total cooperation of the thought-pole and the life-pole, the sign of person who is integrated and well-balanced.

8.

OCCULT POWERS

The Maderanertal was absolutely peaceful when I hiked through it in the summer of 1934. At that time, the Turk's-cap lily, *Lilium martagon*, was still growing wild there. And in the window of a little shop in Bristen lay pieces of rock-crystal, prised out of a nearby brook. I took one or two home with me and they are now sitting on the mantlepiece in my room as watchers. It is as if they see everything that happens in the room, or absorb the cares of those who enter it and lift their depressions.

Try it for yourself: if you have a small pain anywhere, an upset stomach or an agitated heart, lay a piece of rock-crystal against it. It will dispel the cramp and tension and the disharmonious vibrations. And no wonder, for it consists of pure silica, silicic acid. In homoeopathy, Silicea is the substance with the power to expel from a living body those things that have no right to be there, such as a splinter of tooth left behind after an extraction, a swallowed pin or a poison.

Do you suffer from insomnia or bad dreams? Take your favourite stone to bed, even if it is a sharp-pointed crystal. You will find it works just as well as a bunch of herbs hung over your bed or a hop pillow. Invisible but perceptible forces will surround you and irradiate the place in which you lie.

The forces that reside in stones find a point of application in us, since they have been created according to the same pattern as we ourselves have. They are not like the dangerous chemical tranquillizers which have been extracted in the factory from their natural surroundings away from the company of substances to which they belong.

A house containing stones taken from Nature is charged with power. The stones animate the lives of the occupiers and inspire the thinker at his writing-table. The more recently they have been mined the better. Old stones can be effective if they are worn, for they live just as people do, by giving and taking and by interchanges with other created things. Do not hide them away for too long, but take them out of your jewel box every now and again, speak to them gratefully and praise them for their beauty. And wear them once in a while. They want to be with you and to be loved, or to have notice taken of them at least. A precious stone is like a woman: the more you cherish her the more beautiful she grows.

For a precious stone does not exist in isolation, it has a function to perform. There are electric stones, which mostly give, and magnetic stones, which mostly take; not that they take your life-force but the calamity that threatens you. They take your troubles on themselves. Examples of such magnetic stones are the rose quartz (of Venus) and the amethyst (of Neptune), which sometimes display cracks, which are the wounds received in taking over someone else's heavy lot.

Do I hear someone say that all this is impossible, that it is far-fetched nonsense or imagination? Well, the crack in the stone is not 'imagination' because I define imagination as the making of 'images' of things that have no real existence, and the cracking of the stone is an 'image' of something which has actually taken place—not, in the first place, on the physical plane but in the invisible ether.* Some will understand this better than others, but we shall all come to know it by and by.

---

*The Dutch original has a neat play on words here, by splitting the word *verbeelding* (imagination) into its component parts, *ver-beelding*. I have tried to express the same idea in English in a more round about way.

Translator's note.

9.
HEALING GEMS

The Link

All naturally produced substances possess their own vibrations and powers, and these have been used from earliest times by man for specific ends. The power in each substance manifests itself in response to some incoming cosmic vibration sent out by a heavenly body. Thus, gold responds to the vibrations of the Sun and silver to those of the Moon. Earth, therefore, with all she bears, is a reflection of or analogy to the universe and the same applies to all living planets. *As above, so below* says the ancient adage.

Precious stones are usually composed of more than one substance and their allocation to given cosmic powers then depends on the particular substance and vibration that are most prominent.

People, too, can be divided into types in exactly the same way, and the cosmic powers with most influence on their constitutions and characters may be identified from their horoscopes. On recognizing a common vibration in a planet, a person and a precious stone, one knows which particular stone that person should use to bring him luck (in which case it will serve him as a talisman or luck-bringer) or to ward off trouble (as an amulet) or to prevent or cure disease. Anyone who grasps the essential nature of a person and a stone can intuitively select the correct stone for the person at a given moment (at another time some other stone may be required). The horoscope will serve as a useful control here. It was the famous Greek physician Hippocrates who declared that a doctor who is not an astrologer is not a doctor.

The Method

The use of a precious stone as a healing agent takes various forms.

A fragment of emerald, ruby, lapis lazuli or rock crystal, used to be crushed to a powder, the powder was mixed with a drink and the invalid took the mixture. At an even earlier date, beakers were made of precious stone and a sick person would drink water or wine out of one of these.

The stone imparts its vibrations to the liquid in a very short space of time and its radiations have no difficulty in passing through glass. An enormous force-field is created in a safe where jewels are stored, in a jeweller's shop, in a museum where gemmed ornaments are displayed and by church treasures or crown jewels.

Use is made of this fact in the more refined healing methods such as those employed in the Zeileis Clinic at Gallspach in Austria (not far from Linz). The Clinic was started by the father of the present Dr Zeileis in an old castle, and originally he relied on nothing more than his own innate healing power. His original intention was to use this secluded castle for experimental purposes but he was so inundated with patients that he was forced to build extensions and engage a staff to deal with the thousand patients per day who eventually came to him. Electrical apparatus, which was partly of his own invention and partly imported from America, was employed by him to do what was beyond his own capacity.

His collaborator was the remarkable lady doctor, Dr Maria Rotter, the authoress of books on precious stones. In one of the treatment rooms she placed two rows of small cabinets in which a number of precious stones were set out in a certain arrangement behind glass. Patients for whom the treatment was deemed suitable were made to walk once up and once down between the cabinets, either every day or every other day, according to the nature of their complaints and to the exigencies of the treatment. The said treatment has been praised as very effective. This clinic is still open, and patients who are not bed-ridden can sign in there and stay at one of the many boarding-houses in the little country town of Gallspach, where everything possible is done to enable people to keep to the time-table of the Clinic over a course of several weeks.

The simplest way of exposing oneself to the radiations from a precious stone is to wear it against the naked body, whether one is dressed or undressed. A cut stone is worn decoratively in necklaces or on the forehead, in a ring or bracelet or set in a brooch. In this respect, different stones are best worn in their own special ways, as we shall explain when speaking of the individual stones separately. Generally speaking, it is good to wear the appropriate stone over the place of the diseased organ, perhaps in a little bag made of thin gauze (not plastic) stitched to the underclothing.

Uncut stones are equally suitable for use in healing. They can be bought quite cheaply from dealers or polishers. The best thing for the lover of precious stones to do is to take a trip to *Idar-Oberstein* on the Nahe, a tributary of the Rhine, in West Germany, because that is a major industrial centre for them. It is made up of three small towns, Unterstein, Oberstein and Idar lying in a valley, with a castle in the woods on the mountain. The little city is strung out down the valley and is full of small workshops (where the stones are cut and polished) and of showrooms, etc. Caves can still be visited on the slopes of the mountain in which so much agate, amethyst, etc., was found formerly that there was plenty of work for the entire district. Nowadays, the crude stones are imported from Brazil and the art of polishing and setting them is handed down from father to son.

A precious stone can sometimes help to cure an acute illness. Nevertheless, it acts more on the etheric body of man than on the physical one. Hence the prolonged wearing of the correct stone is recommended for a lasting effect on the constitution and for strengthening those parts which suffer from an innate weakness. The mind is also influenced. For example, if someone is afflicted with a weak heart or a weak solar plexus, these organs can be strengthened by constantly wearing a small piece of rock crystal over the heart or over the solar plexus. At the same time this will strengthen the will. The heart, solar plexus and will are invariably expressions of the vibrations of the Sun and, when the former are weak, so will the Sun itself be in the horoscope (especially when unaspected).

The more precious stones a person wears, the more strongly will they be charged with cosmic forces, which they will radiate out into their surroundings. That is why the monarch used to wear so many jewels, in order to turn himself or herself into a living battery of power for the nation. As is known, some kings and queens were able to cure certain diseases. Thus, the kings of France cured their subjects of goitre by the laying on of hands. This was both inner and outer healing power.

For the same reason the high priest of Israel wore his breastplate with the twelve precious stones in accordance with the twelve signs of the Zodiac and with the twelve planets (both visible and invisible). Anyone who possesses genuine jewels would be wise to wear them rather than to shut them away in a safe while making do with imitations. Why should we deprive our souls and our etheric and physical bodies of the tremendous forces which nature bestows on us in order to invigorate us?

Sympathetic Action

Whereas one sort of precious stone will give life force to an ill person, another will draw out the poison from him. One builds up his resistance, the other removes the disease and takes it over. Of course, the choice of stone will be partly determined by the constitution of the sufferer. People with positive constitutions (yang, odd numbers, hot) can stir themselves to fight the disease, but those with negative constitutions (yin, even numbers, cold) need protection. Anyway, an insight into the nature of the disease and the patient's type together with the help provided by his horoscope, can lead to the correct choice of stone.

By way of assistance we shall list possible applications. The traditionalists often hark back to two medieval churchmen who dabbled in healing with precious stones, namely Marbodius (1037-1125) and Albertus Magnus (1193-1280). However, since the pattern of disease is not the same now as in their days, it is better to avoid too much reliance on tradition when selecting a stone for medical use but instead to base treatment on a thorough knowledge of the essential nature of each gem.

In antiquity and in the Middle Ages many a ruler was afraid of being poisoned, and so not only did he employ a personal food taster but he also had his drinks poured into a goblet made of precious stone which would become discoloured if ever it held poison. Typical of the stones used were topaz, malachite, agate and jacinth. Sometimes a stone of this sort would be dropped into the drink to see if it would show any reaction. The diamond was thought to neutralize poisons. Beautiful cups made of onyx may still be seen in museums.

Stones worn on the body sometimes take harmful substances out of the body or *draw the pattern of disease, pain or misfortune out of the etheric body.* Thus, someone who had been ill for a long time would find that the amethyst they were wearing suddenly cracked and that from that moment they themselves quickly recovered. A rider who was wearing a turquoise ring almost fell with his steed over a precipice while negotiating a narrow mountain path. His horse recovered its footing at the very last moment—but the turquoise had cracked.

But precious stones not only remove harmful things—they also allow the wearer to absorb power from them. Thus, it is well known that ruby and coral will fade when their owner is ill, especially in anaemia. This is why, years ago, the farmer's wives and fisher-women used to wear a fourfold string of red coral fastened with a golden clasp around their necks. The chains and golden casques fitted around their heads and on both sides of the face and shining through the sides of their white-prowed caps and the golden coils sticking up beside their eyes, were not intended in the first place for show but as antennae for the reception of cosmic forces, which in this case were the gold of the Sun and the energizing radiations of Mars, the red planet.

The question will be asked as to how we may recognize the special virtues of the stones. The answer is by studying three main characteristics:

1. Their colouring
2. Their chemical composition
3. The forms of their crystals

The Colours
Since a given stone may come in several colours, our choice will be decided by the colour of the stone and not by its name. Thus there are both yellow and blue sapphires, for example. Now whereas the blue sapphire is decidedly a stone of Taurus with properties of faithfulness, devotion, composure and peace of mind to impart, the yellow sapphire has a more animating effect, strengthening the initiative and provoking to action (Virgo).

Stones can easily be divided between the positive and negative colours:

positive	negative
red, orange, yellow, yellow-green, terracotta, gold	blue-green, blue, purple, brown, grey, silver

in-between shades
green, cognac, liver-brown, beige

Stones with positive colours are Yang and bestow power, stones with negative colours are Yin and absorb poisons and misfortune.

The most powerfully purifying stones are purple, as for example the amethyst, a stone of Pisces, which can free the wearer from poisons and from impure thoughts. The deep red ruby gives energy and passion. It even has coercive power, and in India they call it the 'Lord of all stones'. All green stones, like the emerald, the chrysoprase, the olivine, the aventurine and the jade are harmonizing; they produce equilibrium and promote reconciliation, justice and equity.

In general the effects of the colours are as follows:

Red

Red acts on the heart, the blood and circulation, on sexual desire and on incarnation. Hence, it helps to prevent premature births, heals wounds, staunches bleeding, and helps a person through high fever. It warms, draws blood to the place where the stone is, so sucking any poison up to the skin, relieves cramp and stops the pain of the latter.

Light and dark red act centrifugally, they impel, produce restlessness, combativeness, activity, energy, violence and might. They attract carbon, allow it to expand and let it spread through the body more freely. A red stone should be worn by someone who is dull, sleepy, sickly and anaemic, cold, lethargic, pale and sexless, or by a child that will not grow and sits still in a corner.

Red stones are: ruby, red jasper, blood-red carnelian, blood stone (haematitie), almandine, rhodonite and rhodochrosite, hessonite, magnetite, spinel ruby, pyrope, agate and garnet.

Red belongs to Mars, the lighter shade of Aries and the darker shade (as in garnet and pyrope) to Scorpio. It influences the first chakra.

Orange
Orange is a mixture of the life-drive of red and the cleverness of yellow. It cures a person of earthiness, making him magnanimous and giving him a strong feeling of his own self-importance. Orange suits people who have become slaves to their sense of duty and obligation to others. An orange stone (e.g. an orange jacinth) promotes the digestion and assimilation of food, and the removal of old grievances and the dissolving of stones. It restores suppressed menses, and cures chronic asthma and bronchitis (provided the patient does not smoke).

Orange stones are, for example: topaz, orange jacinth, orange carnelian, fire-opal, heliodor (yellow beryl), padparadschah sapphire.

Orange belongs to Jupiter and influences the second chakra, associated with the spleen and the pancreas.

Yellow
Yellow is the colour of the brain and nerves, of thinking and speaking, of contact making and exchange. It attracts hydrogen, has to do with ingestion, assimilation and building up (anabolism), and promotes mental and physical digestion. It acts on the liver and the solar plexus, expels gas, cures diabetes, purifies and heals the skin and opens its pores. In India it is used to cure leprosy. People who are passive and dreamy are activated by yellow and brought more into the mainstream of life. Yellow rouses, gives tempo, strengthens the nerves, makes a person cheerful and overcomes fatigue.

Yellow stones are: citrine, topaz and yellow diamond for Gemini and yellow sapphire and yellow carnelian for Virgo. Yellow belongs to Mercury and influences the third chakra.

Gold
Gold-coloured stones strengthen the heart. Examples are cat's eye, tiger's eye, gold topaz, chrysoberyl, pyrites and sunstone. They are antispasmodic and also give self-confidence. The colour of gold belongs to the Sun and acts on the fourth chakra.

Pink
Pink stones, like the rose quartz help to arouse tender feelings of love; they belong to Venus and her sign Taurus. They put people into an affectionate frame of mind and a childlike state of happiness. Their action is on the thymus gland and their manganese content promotes creative thinking.

Green

Green, as a mixture of warm yellow and cold blue, is the colour of balance, of Libra the Scales. It gives quiet self-control and maturity, well-considered judgement and refinement. It attracts helium out of the atmosphere.

Green stones have a favourable effect on the heart, kidneys, the cerebellum and the female organs. They can help to cure influenza, neuralgia, migraine, venereal diseases and cancer and normalize blood pressure. They act on the fourth chakra.

The full-bodied leaf green and the soft spring green work best. On the other hand, poison green must certainly not be employed. Yellow-green, lime green, olive green, khaki, pea-soup green, make for cheerfulness, practical skill, economy, hospitality and sociability. Green is good for stomach complaints. It belongs to Cancer.

Excellent *green stones* are: olivine or peridot (the stone called chrysolite in nature), serpentine (yellow green), aventurine uvarovite (calcium chrome garnet), chrysoprase (apple green), emerald (for the eyes), jade (light green), nephrite (for the kidneys), alexandrite.

Peacock blue

Peacock blue or green blue, also called turquoise, is a mixture of green and blue and is a quite dangerous colour, mainly suitable for neutralizing too much internal orange. It is a colour which can make people over-sensitive, irritable, sharply critical, very intuitive and difficult to get on with. It agrees with Aquarius, the sign of Uranus. It is the preference of eccentrics and suits golden or copper-coloured hair.

Like green it is good for the eyes and for cutification.

Peacock blue stones are: the turquoise, malachite, amazonite, aquamarine.

Blue

Blue is the cool and cooling colour *par excellence*, calming to the mind and calling us into the far distances, the colour that brings sleep and gives a serious and believing attitude. It is the colour of Taurus and of Virgo (the pure maiden who serves others). Blue is connected with washing, hygiene and sobriety, with abstinence and defence. Blue lowers the blood pressure, inhibits the vitality, soothes pain, attracts oxygen and encourages the production of white blood cells (another example of defence).

Blue stones have an antiseptic and disinfectant action, and cooling effect on abscesses and ulcers and in fever. They temper an excess of red such as is found in rashes and inflammations and in anything of a fiery nature. They are good against aphthae, dysentery and cholera, for stings, haemorrhages and painful menstruation, and for nervous headaches, insomnia, palpitation and vomiting.

Blue encourages chastity, dutifulness, diligence, conscientiousness. It acts on the fifth chakra (at throat level) and cures throat troubles (cf. the blue neck of Shiva after drinking the world poison).

Blue stones are the blue sapphire (which ties a tight love-knot), lapis lazuli, sodalite, azurite, galenite (a lead ore), labradorite, moonstone and blue calcite.

Indigo

This is dark blue with a hint of violet in it. It is a purple blue, the colour of fresh red cabbage, suitable for older women, because they value wisdom and understanding and pure religious thoughts.

Indigo strengthens and heals the sense organs, especially the eyes and ears and also promotes 'clear' seeing (clairvoyance), hearing (clairaudience) and smelling. It can make one insensible to pain and is necessary for occult practices and the curing of mental illnesses such as schizophrenia. An indigo stone can help in the exorcism of evil spirits, and helps in the fits of infants, in all complaints of the air passages, in facial diplegia, delirium tremens, melancholy and hypochondria, mania, hallucinations, dementia, hysteria, epilepsy, Parkinson's disease and in all derangements of the thinking capacity.

Blue or *red purple* stones are the spinel ruby from Ceylon and the pyrope for example.

Purple

Purple or violet is a balanced mixture of blue and red. It is the colour of purification and mysticism, of spiritual things and of the church. It elevates the soul and cures neuroses. The blue component cleanses and the red component fortifies. As a synthesis of what is practical and what is spiritual, it is a help to artists, who have trouble in reconciling these two aspects of life. It calms and prevents their outbursts, helps them to sleep and alleviates their headaches. All that need be done is to stroke the forehead and temples with the purple amethyst. To do so will benefit all troubles of the head, such as meningitis, falling hair, concussion, cataract, and running colds or a blocked nose.

Purple acts on the seventh chakra, above the crown. It belongs to Neptune and its Sign Pisces. The manganese content gives the stone its purple colour. Manganese is essential to creative thinking. Sometimes it is responsible for a pinker tone, as in rose quartz, almandine and rhodochrosite.

White

Since white is not strictly speaking a 'colour', white stones act in a way that is special to themselves. In accordance with the doctrine of signatures,* they are said to promote lactation in mothers who are breast-feeding their babies. Thus in Italy, for example, a so-called *pietro latte* or milk stone, such as the white chalcedony, the white serpentine or the white agate, is worn for this purpose. White opals with their mother-of-pearl sheen are to be avoided, however, as they are deceitful or treacherous to those who rely on them.

White has an affinity with the etheric body in man and strengthens it and keep it clean. It belongs to the Moon.

Black

A completely black onyx and the gleaming black jet belong to Saturn and promote abstract thought in man, also seriousness and self-control, dryness and mortification, emaciation and preservation. These stones bestow resilience and great staying-power. Old ladies' dresses used to be smothered in jet in former days.

Black is the symbol of matter in contrast to white as the symbol of spirit.

Brown

Brown stones usually have a reddish tint, as do carnelian and silex. Others, such as smoky quartz and titanite (also known as sphene), are pure brown. Topaz can sometimes be brown in colour too. Agate and sardonyx are a magnificent brown. The iridescent cat's eye and tiger's eye are golden brown in colour. Onyx can be a mixture of black and brown.

---

*The doctrine of signatures states that something about the appearance of a herb, stone or other natural object will suggest its usefulness, especially for healing or, according to the Mystics, to teach spiritual truth.

Translator's note.

Brown stabilizes and consolidates and is therefore good for all who tend to be flighty, restless and superficial. It makes people reliable and practical, solid and steady.

Beige—cognac—liver colour
These are varieties of brown but with more lightness and luxury. In sand colour and cream the strength of brown is completely lacking.

10.
HEALING GEMS IN HISTORY

Anyone who wishes to delve deeper into the lore of precious stones as handed down by tradition will refer to the mediaeval stone-books or *Lapidaria*, in which information from the Far East as well as from Greece and Rome has been carefully collected and illustrated by many striking examples from practice. They contain highly complicated prescriptions for remedies meant to serve as panaceas against all types of poison and infection, remedies which would be kept in every well-to-do household. Indeed, those who could afford it would dose themselves with some such potion every morning by way of precaution. For example, there was the so-called *Electuarium ex Gemmis Johannis Mesuae*, a confection of herbs and precious stones. In addition to twenty species of plant, this also contained red coral, scrapings of ivory, amber, musk, gold-leaf and silver; powdered pearls, sapphire, jacinth, carnelian, garnet and emerald.

In the latter half of the seventeenth century the *Confectio Hyacinthi* still stood high in popular esteem. This was an expensive antidote made from ten herbs in addition to red coral, Armenian bole (red clay from Armenia), *terra sigillata* (Ancient Roman pottery, red or black), scrapings of ivory, musk, amber, gold leaf and silver, sapphire, emerald, topaz, pearls and jacinth.

Mithridatium and *Theriaca* were famous antidotes in antiquity, especially employed by princes.

Jacob van Maerlant, in his book *Der Naturen Bloeme* (The Flowers of Nature), gave a list of sixty-six healing stones. Included were stones of animal origin, such as the *allectorius*, a stone that in five years grows in the liver of a capon and is crystal clear; the *borax* or *crapaudina*, that is to say the toadstone, said to be found in the head of a toad; the *ceraunius*, formed by lightning as it strikes the ground; the *chelidonius*, given by the swallow to its blind young in order to make them see; the *dracontides* which had to be cut from the head of a living dragon, and the *ligurius*, that was formed from the urine of the lynx. Another well-known book was the *Gemmarum et Lapidum Historia*, by the Dutchman, Anselmus Boëtius de Boodt, personal physician to the Emperor Rudolph II in Prague. It came out in Hanau in 1609.

Apart from gems and animal stones, the healing power of the Earth itself has attracted attention since the earliest ages, and even today we use kaolin and healing earth to draw out poisons and to cool and soothe inflammations. It is fact of nature that earth and water are magnetic or attractive in quality.

In antiquity the clay of the Greek island of Lemnos was celebrated for its curative properties. The Roman doctor Galen tells how he made a special trip there. In the town of Hephestios there stood a hill where the priestesses of the temple dug out the healing earth after they had brought a thank offering of wheat and barley. Back at the temple, the red earth was mixed with water and allowed to stand for a while. The water and the impurities which had risen to its surface were then decanted and the sediment left behind was kneaded into round biscuits and marked with the stamp of the goddess Diana. They were then known by the name of sealed earth or *terra sigillata*. Galen returned to Rome with some 20,000 tablets. When mixed with vinegar, this earth was used on wounds and on the bites of venomous creatures and, if anyone had been bitten by a mad dog, he took it in wine as an internal remedy.

The Armenian bole, mentioned in one of the prescriptions given above, was a clay prized for its drying effect in diarrhoea, haemorrhages and consumption. It was also reputed to heal the plague. This clay together with *terra sigillata* was laid on burns to prevent the formation of blisters and to promote rapid healing. A white earth was found in Lemnos at the town of Repondi, known as the *terra Lemnia*. According to a book written in 1655, the Greek inhabitants used to dig it up at a solemn ceremony once a year on the 6 August. The fragrant earth was taken out of the ground, with the permission of the Turkish rulers, only during the six hours when the Sun was still in the east.

After this it was washed and, after the excess water had been removed, was pressed into tablets bearing the seal of the Sultan and sent to Constantinople (now known as Istanbul) as 'the very best remedy for the plague and erysipelas'. *Terra sigillata* used to be on sale in Holland stamped with the coat of arms of Leyden.

Other types of healing earth are found on Zealand in Denmark, near a spring consecrated to St Helena, in Silesia and in Bohemia. The last named was used for making beakers and pots which were supposed to impart their curative properties to whatever was put in them.

11.

CRYSTALLINE FORMS

Six systems have been identified in the world of crystals:

1. *The regular or cubic system*
These crystals have three axes of equal length set at right angles to one another. In other words they are cubic.

The cubic form is the most earthy of all, being the lowest and latest form of densification. In materialistic eras people build in cubes or rectangular blocks, such as we see going up all round us today. Four is the number of matter. The right-angle makes things hard and is the expression of permanent rigidity. It leads to conflict (cf. the square aspect in astrology) due to its unyielding egoism and lust for power. It is the form of Mars and the cube is formed by Mars and Saturn (i.e. the right-angle plus the square).

Examples: *garnet, pyrites, common salt, galenite.*

2. *The tetragonal system*
These crystals have two axes of equal length and a third of unequal length all set at right-angles. They are shaped like a beam crowned with a four-sided pyramid (composed of course of four triangles).

This is a combination of the four and the three, as seen in the design of Grecian temples, in which the square or rectangular base has a rectangular front with pillars supporting the triangular pediment. The street-doors of the houses in Greek villages are usually still constructed in this way. This means three over four, or spirit over matter. A shape like this attracts the forces of light through its triangles. The classical house with a gable roof and its triangular cross-section attracts spiritual force for the benefit of its occupants, in contrast to the house with a flat roof. In this system we have the activity of Mars (four) and Jupiter (three).

Examples: *zircon, rutile, cassiterite (tin-stone).*

3. *The hexagonal system*
These crystals have three mutually similar axes in the same plane set at 120 degrees and a fourth axis of different length lying at right-angles to this plane. Thus a six-sided prism is formed, and six denotes man on earth.

The hexagon and the six-pointed star made of two interpenetrating triangles, known as the Star of David, stand for the harmonious individual, interested both in the things of matter and of the body (the triangle with its point turned downwards) and in the things of the spirit (the triangle with its point turned upwards). Such a person is integrated, with his vitality-pole and his thought-pole working together. The bee, which spends its life work-sharing in the bee state, builds hexagonal cells for the larvae and for the storage of honey. Living in hexagonal structures should guarantee a peaceful society. The six stands for peace and is a representative of Venus; the long crystals have Mercury in them too. Think of the quiet rhythm of the hexameter in poetry, with its six beats in every line.

Examples: the *quartzes* (rock crystal), *beryl, calcite, tourmaline* and *cinnabar.*

4. *The rhombic system*
These crystals have three mutually unequal axes at right-angles to one another. This allows all sorts of variety in shape, as in the sulphur crystals with their adjacent trapezia and pyramidal ends. They are the forms of the Sun and they are encountered in sulphur because it is *solfer* or Sun-bearer, and in the olivine which has left the Sun as light and has congealed into a meteor stone and entered our atmosphere. These are remote forms, heavenly forms.

Examples: *sulphur, olivine, celestine, staurolite.*

5. *The monoclinic system*
These crystals have three mutually unequal axes, two of which are set

at an oblique angle to one another. The third axis is perpendicular to the plane of the other two. Saturn and Pluto work here with their hidden light.

Examples: *gypsum, mica, augite, epidote, hornblende.*

6. *The triclinic system*

These crystals have three mutually unequal axes set at oblique angles to one another. Like Uranus, they are rather capricious.

Examples: *amazonite, rhodonite, chalcanthite.*

12.

THE CHEMICAL COMPOSITION OF PRECIOUS STONES

Silicic Acid

All quartzes and indeed nearly all precious stones (except for the diamond, the rhodochrosite and the chrysoberyl) consist mainly of silicic acid (which dissociates into water and silica). This substance, which belongs to Sagittarius, has the property of attracting light and driving out evil, a property that makes precious stones good things to wear generally speaking. Silicic acid imparts self-confidence, strengthens the back (especially the intervertebral discs), promotes the discharge of water, pus and all superfluous and undesirable materials and protects the nerves.

Rock crystal consists entirely of silicic acid and is therefore first choice for the above applications.

Magnesium

Many stones contain magnesium (magnesia), a substance that strengthens the heart and liver, relaxes the body and relieves cramp, soothes pain and benefits the nerves. It belongs to Leo. Stones that are rich in magnesium can be laid on any spot suffering from cramp or pain.

Examples are olivine, serpentine, pyrope, almandine and spinel ruby.

Aluminium

Although the particles of aluminium we ingest with food that has been cooked in aluminium ware must be regarded as poisons to be avoided, the aluminium in precious stones is just as beneficial as the Alumina (oxide of aluminium) given homoeopathically. It belongs to Neptune and Pisces and fortifies those who are thin and debilitated, who become dizzy when they run or bend and sometimes suffer from paralysis, degenerative processes and psychoses. It is good for those who find it difficult to digest their food (dyspepsia) and are worse in dry cold weather.

Aluminium is found in such stones as the ruby, sapphire, serpentine, pyrope, almandine, tourmaline, turquoise, epidote and moonstone.

Manganese

This element, related to iron, is good for anaemic people who have a tendency towards paralysis and exaggerated reflexes (Parkinson's disease, multiple sclerosis), and also for those who do a lot of singing or speaking and are always having to clear their throats of mucus. Manganese encourages creative thinking.

Rhodochrosite consists entirely of manganese. The element is also found in rose quartz, amethyst and almandine.

Iron

Stones with an iron content are good to be worn by anaemic individuals and in fever, congestion, inflammation and haemorrhage. A necklace of blood-red coral is an old remedy. Other stones which should be mentioned are haematite (bloodstone), magnetite, marcasite, limonite, pyrites, sierite, andradite, pyrrhotite, chlorite and olivine. Iron belongs to Mars and the Sign of Aries.

Copper

This strengthens the nerves and is good for all sorts of spasms (including asthma and epilepsy), spasm of the heart (myocardial spasm), spasm of the intestines (enterospasm) and multiple sclerosis. Copper belongs to Venus and the Sign of Libra.

It is found in the stones, turquoise, malachite, azurite, pyrites, tabernite and chrysocolla.

Calcium

Calcium stiffens the bones and gives resistance against emotions. It is present in all kinds of stones (fluorspar, apatite, epidote, uvarovite, andradite) and is best employed in a pearl necklace. Calcium belongs to Saturn and the Sign of Capricorn.

Fluorine is found in the topaz and in apatite.
Chromium in the emerald and in uvarovite.
Nickel in chrysoprase and serpentine.
Boron in tourmaline.
Potassium in the Moonstone.

13.

THE PREPARATION OF GEMS

Polishing

Just as a child looks for pretty pebbles on the beach, so ancient man took pleasure in the finely-marked stones he discovered. He saw how the big rivers wore away the pieces of rock until they were smooth and round and this gave him the idea of grinding and polishing his own stones to improve their appearance and to disclose their inner beauty. His first attempts were made with soft stones and only gradually was the technique developed of grinding the hard ones with abrasive powder prepared from stones that were even harder.

The oldest form of polished gem is the *cabochon* and is convex on one or both sides. It was made by grinding projections. When men began to polish octagonal diamond crystals, faceted *brilliants* which tapered downwards resulted, and then, the points of the natural crystals were removed to give a *table* on top of the gem. When this form was accompanied by terraces cut below the table the *step* variety was produced. The facets were polished by means of a wheel covered in leather and smeared with diamond powder and oil.

Triangular facets occur in brilliants but, in the step cut, the facets lie parallel to one another. It is the fact that light is reflected at different angles within the stone due to the way in which it has been cut that makes the stone sparkle.

Fire

Fire is the name given to the way a ray of light flashes back from the depths of a stone as we turn the latter round. Colourless stones have the most fire, but a lot also depends on room lighting. By far the best form of illumination is that given by many tiny points of light—as found in the candle flame for instance. Picture to yourself for a moment a banquet of olden days held in a hall lit by chandeliers and attended by lovely ladies in all their finest jewellery. Eyes and gems look their best by candlelight!

Brilliance
Brilliance differs from fire. What is more, there is an obvious difference between the brilliance of the diamond and that of glass, resin, wax, metal, grease, silk, etc. When a mixture of gems is being used in ornaments, the type of brilliance must be taken into account. One type will make a pleasing contrast to another.

For example, diamonds combine well with rubies, sapphires or emeralds but not with zircons, because the latter have a diamond-like lustre, whereas rubies, sapphires and emeralds have a brilliance of a similar character to that of glass.

It is a great pity that the crystalline forms of stones are sometimes violated by hasty and ill-advised cutting. Let us leave such mutilated specimens in their museum cases and select stones which are free to express their inner beings because they have retained their natural forms. The form of the diamond for instance, should have an octagonal symmetry.

The Cullinan was a beautiful diamond the size of a man's fist presented to King Edward VII by the Government of South Africa. It was split by the firm of Assher in Amsterdam, long noted for their skill in cutting and polishing diamonds, and various smaller gems were made from it to be set in crowns and sceptres.

Instead of having parts cut away, a large and perfect stone may be split along the cleavage planes of its crystal; it will always divide into pieces similar to itself under impact and even the very particles in its powder will have the same form. Like the scions of the old nobility, it is refined through and through; it is like some perfected variety of flower with a long pedigree, such as the columbine.

A homely illustration of what we mean is the old-fashioned lump of candy which was allowed to crystallize on a piece of thread hanging in sugar solution. If the lump, which was a big crystal, was too large, the housewife would squeeze it between the jaws of the lump-cutter in such a way as to exert pressure along its plane of cleavage. Everyday life was once full of such techniques that informed and educated the mind. A tiny flaw in a stone will often indicate the plane of cleavage which helps to identify the type to which the stone belongs.

Cameo and Intaglio

When stones are composed of differently coloured layers, as is so frequently the case in agate, they can be made into ornaments by carving out a small figure in the uppermost layer so that the lower layer forms a contrasting background.

If the design stands out, e.g. a white head on a red background, we have a *cameo*; if, on the other hand, the design is incised into the lower layer, the result is known as *intaglio*. The stones of signet rings have been made like this from of old, so that when the impression is made in sealing wax it will stand out. The technique is extremely ancient and signet staffs and signet rings have been found in very old graves in Chaldea and Egypt. Ancient Rome was the world centre for intaglio work; for skilled engravers were brought back to the capital from conquered lands. They worked on sapphires and emeralds, on jasper, carnelian and lapis lazuli, the favourite stone of the ancient Egyptians.

Sometime in the seventh century A.D., people in Rome began to dig up old treasures, and these often consisted of representations of Greek and Roman gods in this intaglio work. By that time, Christianity had become the official religion and so Aphrodite and Eros were put on sale as pictures of Mary and the child Jesus, a satyr became Peter, Jupiter was taken for St Oswald, and Dionysus, the god of wine, was converted into John the Baptist. Hermes was regarded as the archangel Michael, and Leda with the swan decorated a reliquary shrine housing an alleged tooth of the apostle Peter!

Colour

The art of polishing a precious stone in such a way as to bring out as much of its colour as possible, was very highly developed in ancient India. Indian princes counted their riches mainly in precious stones and did not take kindly to losing much weight of stone by polishing. Therefore the polishers went to work very carefully, since their lives could depend on it!

The Laws of Manu, two thousand years old, give very precise instructions for polishing. It was suggested at one time that Manu was an ambassador from the planet Venus who stayed on Earth long enough to teach human beings all kinds of techniques before boarding his space ship again for the return journey. Ornamental work is especially associated with Venus.

The colour can be imparted to precious stones in different ways. Where the colour is an inherent property of the stone and is evenly diffused throughout it, it is termed *idiochromatic*, as in the lapis lazuli. But when the stone also contains coloured impurities, it is said to be *allochromatic*. A trace of chromium makes an emerald green but a ruby red. If the trace of colouring matter is spread unevenly, the stone will be flecked and the skill of the polisher will be seen in bringing out the best tint.

Even in crowded rooms, stones with a strong colour, such as the emerald, the turquoise, jade and orange sapphire, will attract attention.

Changing the colours of gems by strongly heating them has been practised from early times. In this way, man imitates nature, which has produced so many lovely colours in stones with the enormous temperatures of volcanic eruptions. The amethyst, for instance, which is essentially a purple type of rock crystal, is heated to 400 degrees to turn it golden yellow. It is then sold as topaz (citrine). Green aquamarine is also heated until it loses its colour but, when it cools down, it turns blue. Pink topaz is made by heating red-brown topaz and so on. In Bangkok, blue zircon is created from the usual form by heating it in charcoal furnaces, and the Cingalese, who found the red-brown zircon on their island, heat it until it is colourless and sell it under the name of Matura diamond. In some parts gems are baked in bread to change their colours.

Iridescence, or change of colour with position, is an especially beautiful effect. It is seen in the cat's eye and tiger's eye, for example. In France, it is called *chatoyant* (from *chat* a cat and *œuil* an eye) appropriately enough. This play of light is caused by parallel veining.

Asterism, or the formation of a star of light when a gem is illuminated with a point source of light, is caused during the process of crystallization by all sorts of circumstances. For example, it may be due to microscopic crystals inside a large one. By special cutting, beautiful star jewels can then be obtained, for example in sapphire or rose quartz.

14.

THE STONES IN
THE ROYAL CROWN

From olden days monarchs have been crowned with crowns of gold decorated with precious stones; not simply from the point of view of giving the impression of pomp and circumstance, but from that of symbolism and for the conduction of power.

Just as each individual has a soul and spirit in addition to a body, so each nation with its own language has a national soul and a national spirit. The nation's soul is the joint soul of all its members. In time of need, it expresses itself in a feeling of solidarity and a love of the native land. The national spirit is a higher being or angel, which leads the nation through each stage of its development. Irrespective of the official idolatrous ideas among heathen nations, these are the beings to whom the populace of each country probably thought they were praying while they paid no more than lip-service to the state divinity.*

The king is divinely appointed to be the custodian of the state, the go-between between the national soul and the national spirit. His office is to bring the power of the national spirit to the people. Ancient kings were high priests also (the separation of church and state only takes place during rationalistic eras).

---

*In this case I have paraphrased freely. The original reads: 'Irrespective of the official religious ideas, each nation worships its own divinity and intends that divinity when the official god is worshipped in the state church and at state ceremonies. The words "God be with us" on Dutch florins is an example of this.' However, Christians and Muslims, whose faith transcends national boundaries, would deny this.   *Translator's note.*

At the time of a coronation, a sacred marriage is contracted between the national spirit and the monarch on the one hand and between the monarch and the people on the other hand. From that time onwards, it is assumed that the national spirit will pour forth its power on the people through the person of the sovereign, bestowing health and prolificity, favourable weather and bountiful harvests. Of course, there were times of bad harvests, famine or epidemics when the people put their king to death, because he had wilfully neglected his duty so they thought.

In some countries people believed that the monarch had been given the power to heal by the national spirit. Thus it was believed that the King of France could cure goitre by the laying on of hands. The soul of the nation has invariably had faith in this power in every kingdom, and so the king or queen would lay the first stone of bridges or buildings in the interests of their subjects, because it was expected that the power would then be transmitted to the whole structure and its function.

The king or queen, like our own Queen Elizabeth,* who rules *Dei gratia* (by the grace of God), has the power to heal people as one of her functions regardless of her personality. Therefore those who are aware of these things do not consider the personality really important. Indeed, people would really prefer to do without a monarch who has so many of his own ideas that these are liable to hinder the transmission of the power or to lend it a certain colouring. King Edward VIII, who was never crowned and abdicated to become the Duke of Windsor rather than forego an unpopular marriage, was a monarch of this character. He was loved for his personality but was unfit to remain king (from the point of view we are considering now) because he wanted to make so many changes.

The power which is poured out at the coronation on the head of the monarch in response to his subject's prayers is seen as a golden light. It is pictured in the gold of the crown; especially when the national spirit is seen as a servant of the great Sun spirit. Gold is a great conductor of the Sun force, the bringer of life, happiness and prosperity. In other words, it is practically the best conductor.

The gems in the crown conduct the powers of the planetary spirits (or archangels), who carry out the initiatives of the solar spirit. During the coronation, the monarch should be surrounded by ministers as rep-

---

*The original text says Queen Juliana, but the remarks about King Edward VIII are the same as in the Dutch.   *Translator's note.*

resentatives of the planetary spirits, each wearing the appropriate precious stones. The coronets worn by the English nobility on state occasions point in this direction.

Nevertheless, the precious stones are usually set in the royal crown itself in order that the powers it attracts can later be bestowed on the ministers by the king or queen. Thus, wearing the crown turns the monarch into a powerful battery of force. Therefore, in olden days, the king and queen had to spend a great deal of time doing nothing else than sitting on their golden thrones with bejewelled golden crowns on their heads and the sceptre and orb in either hand (representing the male and female forces: yang and yin). In this way they could radiate force from the centre of the kingdom, the heart of the nation. There was a continuous reception from above and distribution below.

The exception proves the rule, and there have been crowns that were not made of gold. For example the Lombard queen Theodelinde, who, in spite of her sweet-sounding name was an energetic and powerful ruler who compelled her subjects to give up the Arian heresy and return to the yoke of Rome, had an iron crown made for herself. This was adorned with emeralds, sapphires and pearls and for a thousand years it was kept in Monza, Italy (just north of Milan). In 1797 Napoleon took the crown back with him to Paris, where no one noticed that all the gems and pearls with one exception had been torn out of it and replaced by imitations of glass and nacre. The iron crown of Lombardy is now back in Monza. How clearly Theodelinde must have seen that it was not gold that suited her but the martial metal iron, the image and means of violence.

The *crown of Charlemagne* was made of gold and richly set with precious stones. It was topped by a cross bearing a crest of gems. This crown can now be seen in Vienna.

The so-called *Crown of the Andes* is preserved in the USA. After King Atahualpa, the last Inca of Peru, had been murdered by the Spanish invader Pizarro, a young Spanish nobleman, Sebastian Benalcazar, was appointed governor of Quito and later became bishop of the Spanish settlement in the old Inca city of Popayan. In 1590 a plague raged in the land but Popayan escaped it and the bishop, who had invoked the Virgin Mary for protection, decided to present her with a very beautiful crown by way of a thanks offering. Noble ladies gave up the jewels that had been stolen from the Inca aristocracy and, in 1593, a start was made on making the crown. The work took six years. The crown itself was made from a hundred pounds of gold and it was decorated with 453 emeralds taken from Atahualpa's treasure-chamber. The biggest stone came from his own crown jewels; it was a 45-carat emerald and was chosen as the central point, while seventeen large pendants hung down from the curved supports. When it was completed it was solemnly placed on the head of the image of the Virgin Mary in the cathedral. At the approach of pirates, however, it was hidden in the primeval forest by special guardians: the Brother-hood of the Immaculate Conception.

The golden circlet worn on the brow of Atahualpa himself was concealed by his people and now, after three and a half centuries, it has been handed down to a young Indian living in the inaccessible valleys of the Andes in N.W. Peru, who is seen by his people as the future deliverer who will drive out the Spaniards and those of mixed blood.

The *Imperial crown of the Holy Roman Empire* contained an opal mined in Hungary, which was called the orphanus (the orphan) because it had no predecessors of a similar beauty. Its appearance was that of 'pure white snow shining through the colour of red wine'. This stone was said to protect the honour of the monarch who wore it. Sovereigns were constantly striving for possession of the Orphanus and many a robbery and murder was perpetrated on account of it. The story goes that it finally destroyed its wearer by one last burst of energy, and the stone itself also dried up, disintegrated and crumbled to dust.

The magnificent *crown of Louis XV of France* contained the famous *Sancy diamond*, a stone with such a long and adventurous career, that a whole book could be written on it. It now sparkles in a tiara owned by the Astor family.

However, costly jewels were not left undisturbed in the crowns they originally adorned; the awe in which they were held on account of their great power eventually gave way to a shrewd idea of their market value. Throughout the whole modern era, crown jewels have been pawned to raise massive loans for financing wars between rival princes. Gems have been transferred from royal treasure chests to bankers' vaults then back again to the royal treasure chests, only to be reused as pledges in process of time. Since they were so often bartered, the aura surrounding them became sullied by the dirty politics of power. The more that rulers strove (either on their own initiative or under the guiding hands of their mistresses) for power and glory, to the detriment of the true dignity of their position, the more they misused their precious stones for these base ends. They defiled the purity of the stones even as they destroyed the integrity of their own souls.

Thus, as we may well imagine, the stones themselves had very adventurous careers. At one time they would be glittering in a royal diadem, at another they would be locked away in the safe of some bank and at another they were being smuggled across a border in the heel of a shoe. They were stolen, sold, bartered, given in dowries and exchanged between politicians. The English and French crown jewels often found their way to Holland as securities for loans. Queen Henrietta Maria smuggled a good deal of jewellery to her native France in order to buy muskets and gunpowder for her beleaguered husband, Charles I. The celebrated *Regent diamond*, formerly known as the *Pitt* because it had once belonged to William Pitt's grandfather, was pawned for cavalry equipment in 1790, and the three great balas rubies of France: the Côte de Bretagne, La Romaine and the Oeuf de Naples, frequently travelled to and fro to replenish the treasury.

There is an amusing story about the secret transfer of the crown jewels from *Hanover*. In 1866 the Prussians made a surprise attack on the kingdom of Hanover; the blind king, George V, just managed to escape but had to leave behind his valuables. While the Prussians watched the gates, the royal household packed the crown jewels and an entire service of gold and silver for 2000 persons in empty wine vats. The vats were rolled through an old subterranean passage to a church which had been taken over as a warehouse by a wine merchant. The merchant dispatched the vats by train to Vienna and eventually they were shipped to England. There remained the personal jewellery of the queen, which was initially hidden in the Lord Chamberlain's garden, together with the crown, sceptre and sword of state. Having become uneasy about them, those in the know dug them up again one dark night, concealed them in the linings of their winter-coats and took them to the family crypt. After looking round for a while, they found room for them in the coffin of a young prince and hid them there. The Prussians offered a big reward to anyone who would betray the hiding place, but no one came forward. Nevertheless the situation was so hazardous that the court decided to take the jewels over to England.

A picnic was organized and the crown and jewels were packed in hampers under the eatables, while the swords were put inside gun-covers; though one for which no gun-cover was available was stuck down the trouser-leg of one of the picnicers, who had to feign lameness for the occasion. When they were deep in the forest, the ladies disappeared inside a hunting-box one by one in order to pin necklaces to their petticoats or rings to the inside of their blouses and bodices. The tiaras vanished under their bustles, but the royal crown itself was too large and heavy for this mode of concealment. The stately Countess Kielmannsegg placed it on her head and tied her black lace bonnet over it. And so the company travelled to Vienna and all came safe to England.

Since precious stones represent more or less the same value in all the big cities of the world, they are particularly useful for refugees to take with them as a compact form of capital, especially as they are small enough to be hidden easily—even inside the body!

Some famous stones have made incredible journeys, yet they can be identified by the extremely finely engraved names of their successive possessors. An example is the *Timur ruby*, which bears the following legend under six long Arab and Indian royal names: 'This is that ruby, among the 25,000 jewels of the king of kings Sultan Sahib Sani, which came here from Hindustan in the year 1154.' The Timur ruby was mined somewhere in India and was among the treasures of the sultans of Delhi until the city was taken by the savage invader, Timur Leng of Samarkand who, to celebrate his victory, had a pyramid built of the skulls of those he had slaughtered. The stone remained in the family of Timur Leng (more familiarly known as Tamerlane) until it passed to the Persian Shah, Abbas I, who used it to buy the goodwill of the powerful Grand Mogul Jehangir. On the one hand these Oriental rulers were appallingly cruel and yet on the other hand they were very advanced culturally. Thus Jehangir's father, the mighty Akbar, assembled Brahmins, Moslems and Jesuits at his court in order to hear them debate, and then he attempted to create a religion which would be a synthesis of their three faiths. His son engraved the name of his famous father on the stone and when his wife protested at the desecration of its beauty, he replied, 'This stone will more certainly transmit my name to posterity than would any written chronicle. The race of Tamerlane shall pass away but so long as there remains one king in the world, this stone will be in his possession!'

Jehangir had many mosques built, granted trading rights to the Dutch East India Company, and kept himself informed of political conditions in East and West. In 1627, possession of the stone passed to his son Jehan, who had the Taj Mahal built. To hold audience he sat on the Peacock Throne (which was smothered in jewels to the value of 6,000,000 gold crowns) with the Timur in a necklace. He had his own name engraved on it, adding the words: 'The second lord of the lucky conjunction'.

Shah Jehan had all his male relatives put to death in order to safeguard his tenure of the throne, but was himself imprisoned by Auranzeb his son, who then in 1627 possessed himself of the Peacock Throne and the royal treasures. This man was so cruel that he concealed an iron claw in his glove and if anyone displeased him he would suddenly tear out the unfortunate person's intestines with it. Yet he was a serious scholar and a kindred spirit as far as his interest in precious stones is concerned. When the great French jeweller Tavernier visited him, the latter was permitted to hold even the famed Grand Mogul diamond in his hand.

Auranzeb was succeeded by several other occupants of the Peacock Throne until, in 1739, Nadir Shah invaded India from Persia and took back to his homeland not only the Peacock Throne but also all the crown jewels; among them the Timur ruby, the 'tribute of the world'. For fear of being overthrown, Nadir Shah had his son's eyes put out, but was eventually assassinated by his bodyguard. His weak son, Shah Shusha, was imprisoned by enemies and tortured in an attempt to make him reveal where the Timur, the Koh-i-noor and other renowned stones were hidden. Having been rescued by the Shah of Afghanistan, he gave him the Timur as a mark of gratitude. Unfortunately his noble rescuer was robbed of it by a covetous neighbour, King Ranjit Singh, who was in turn defeated by the English in 1849; after which the East India Company offered its services so that the jewels, including the Timur, could be taken from Lahore and shipped to England for presentation to Queen Victoria. Surrounded by brilliants, the famous ruby now hangs from a necklace occasionally worn by Queen Elizabeth II. And so, after passing through so many cruel hands and after having been the cause of so many murders, it appears to have found peace.

15.
A LIST OF THE HEALING PROPERTIES OF STONES

A

Allergy	— zircon (jacinth)
Asthma	— amber, chrysoberyl, cat's eye, tiger's eye, malachite

B

Biliousness	— jasper
Bladder trouble	— coral, heliotrope, jasper, jade
Bleeding	— chalcedony, chrysoprase, haematite, rock crystal, sapphire
Blood disease	— amethyst
Blood poisoning	— carnelian
Bowel cramp	— cat's eye
Bronchitis	— pyrites, rutilated quartz (needle stone)
Burns	— amethyst

C

Childbirth	— agate, chrysoprase, heliotrope, jacinth, jade
Coldness (to warm)	— topaz
Colic	— coral
Colour blindness	— amethyst
Consumption (pulmonary)	— moonstone

D

Depression	— chalcedony, garnet, lapis lazuli
Diarrhoea	— rock crystal
Dizziness	— rock crystal
Dropsy	— amethyst
Drunkenness	— amethyst

E

Ear trouble	— amber, onyx
Enterospasm (bowel cramp)	— cat's eye
Epilepsy	— jasper
Evil eye (to avert)	— amber, carnelian, cat's eye, hawk's eye, tiger's eye, turquoise
Eyes, watery	— onyx
Eyesight problems	— agate, amethyst (colour blindness), aquamarine, beryl, chrysolite, coral, emerald, magnetite, malachite, obsidian, aventurine

F

Falls (to prevent)	— tourmaline
Fever	— carnelian, ruby
Forgetfulness	— emerald
Fracture	— magnetite

G

Glands (swollen)	— aquamarine
Goitre	— amber

H

Haemorrhage	— chalcedony, chrysoprase, haematite, rock crystal, sapphire
Haemorrhoids	— heliotrope
Hair problems	— agate, aventurine, lapis lazuli, onyx
Hearing problems	— agate, onyx
Heart trouble	— agate, beryl, chrysolite, garnet, onyx

I

Infection	— amber, amethyst, carnelian, sardonyx

Insomnia	— amethyst, jacinth, padparadschah sapphire, sapphire, topaz

K

Kidney trouble	— nephrite, rock crystal

L

Lactation (to promote)	— chalcedony, rock crystal, white agate, white serpentine
Leg cramp	— haematite
Liver trouble	— aquamarine, beryl, jasper, topaz

M

Malaria	— amber
Menstrual disorders	— malachite
Miscarriage (to prevent)	— ruby
Mouth troubles	— beryl

N

Nervousness	— sapphire, topaz, tourmaline
Neuralgia	— magnetite, carnelian
Nightmare	— carnelian
Nose-bleed	— carnelian, magnetite

P

Pain	— ruby, sardonyx
Phthisis	— moonstone
Piles	— heliotrope
Poisoning	— agate, diamond, jacinth, malachite

R

Rheumatism	— amber, carnelian, malachite

S

Scalds	— amethyst
Sleeplessness	— amethyst, jacinth, sapphire, topaz
Smell (loss of sense of)	— jasper
Sores	— carnelian
Spasms	— carnelian, rock crystal, ruby

Stomach trouble — beryl, heliotrope, jasper

T
Taste (loss of sense of) — topaz
Teeth (to cut) — amber
Throat trouble — beryl
Toothache — aquamarine, malachite

U
Ulceration — onyx

V
Vertigo — rock crystal

W
Whooping cough — coral
Wounds — carnelian

16.

QUARTZES

Rock crystal	Plasma
Agate	Praseolite
Carnelian	Jasper
Onyx	Silex
Chalcedony	Heliotrope
Chrysoprase	Smoky quartz
Amethyst	Cat's eye, hawk's eye, tiger's eye
Aventurine	Rutilated quartz (needle stone)
Opal	Rhinestone
Rose quartz	Obsidian
Citrine	Tektite

The crystalline quartzes include rock crystal, citrine, rose quartz, amethyst, cat's eye, tiger's eye, hawk's eye and chalcedony.

The cryptocrystalline quartzes include carnelian, chrysoprase, plasma, heliotrope, agate, onyx, sardonyx and jasper.

All quartzes consist of silica or silicic acid, the substance that is solid cosmic light, so to speak (spirit in matter), and they are encountered wherever there is striving upwards, idealism, and a rising towards the Sun. For instance, silica occurs in the nodes of the stalks of cereals and grasses. These enable the long hollow stem to stand erect and to straighten up after they have bent before the wind. For exactly the same reason, silica enters into the cartilage of the intervertebral discs found in our backbones, enabling us to bow to fate where necessary and then to hold our heads high once more.

Silica also occurs in the lenses of our eyes and is used in glass-making. It strives after clarity, transparency and truth.

The Earth's crust consists partly of the hard igneous rock granite. It has four components: quartz, feldspar, mica and hornblende. Feldspar gives it its colour and mica gives it its shine. Hornblende is dark. And so we have light, colour, lustre and darkness all together, and we shall see how the precious stones are formed from combinations of these factors.

There are completely transparent stones such as rock crystal, which have an affinity with the human spirit.

There are translucent stones such as rose quartz and citrine, which possess colour and belong to the soul of man.

Finally, there are the so-called opaque, compact stones such as jasper, carnelian and onyx, which belong to the physical body of man.

It is easy to see a parallel here with the Signs of the Zodiac and the four elements; where transparent stones belong to the fire signs, translucent stones to the air and water signs and opaque stones to the earth signs.

Rock Crystal

Rock crystal consists of silicic acid or silica and crystallizes in completely transparent, uncoloured hexagonal prisms. When the fluid solution runs into mountain caves it gradually crystallizes into these crystals. For centuries it used to be thought that they were made of ice which had lost the power to melt. In the Middle Ages it was often mistaken for diamond.

If a rock crystal contains inclusions of water or air, it becomes *iris quartz* or *rainbow quartz*, which has a marvellous play of colours. Queen Josephine had a piece of jewellery cut out of one.

For a long time the Swiss Alps were the most important source of beautiful large rock crystals. People used to go looking for them there in the late summer, and were known as Strahlers. The really lucky ones found a crystal cave, which might contain tons of saleable crystal. For example, a famous crystal cave was found in 1719 in the Vorderen Zinkenstock. It is still accessible from the Grimselhospiz. There was also the Sandbalmhöhle in the Göschenertal, discovered in 1700, which can be visited from Wickie. In the summer of 1868 there was found near the town of Guttannen, north of the Furkaweg, a huge cave containing thousands of dark coloured rock crystal, the so-called *morion*. Remarkable pieces of this may be seen in Bern museum.

Beautiful useful objects and ornaments have been made from rock crystal from the oldest times. Thus two vases cut from rock crystal were found in an Egyptian tomb. Splendid bowls and chandeliers of crystal were manufactured in Italy in the Middle Ages, and specimens are on view in the British Museum. An end to all this was put by the Bohemian glass industry which, after 1650, began to market an equally fine but much cheaper type of crystal ware. However, ornaments and paper-weights of crystal are still being made and the large crystal balls used by clairvoyants to see etheric images of future events are among them. These crystal balls have to be so transparent that it is impossible to say whether they are stationary or rolling slightly. The Ancient Romans used to use such balls for cooling their hot hands in summer, because rock crystal is a very good conductor of heat and the heat of the hands was quickly conveyed over the whole ball. In China and Japan, these crystal balls are employed in public worship.

In another connection, rock crystal is used by industry for optical articles such as prisms, lenses, echelon gratings for spectrometers, microscopes and saccharimeters. In radio-engineering laboratories, vibrating plates are prepared from it for ultrasonic transmitters and regulators. Rock crystal melts readily in an oxyhydrogen flame and in this way quartz glass is manufactured for test tubes, sun lamps and mercury lamps. Also, extremely thin threads are made from melted quartz for the suspension of small magnets, etc. in sensitive measuring instruments.

The rock crystals found in Northern Ireland and certain parts of Ireland are called *God stones*, and they were buried with the dead, a custom also observed by the American Indians, because rock crystal bears the divine light in it, it attracts the soul towards the light.

The rock crystal is as clear as water and therefore was used as a rain-maker (for instance, a farmer would bury a piece in his field). The Chinese use rock crystal to relieve their thirst on a journey through the desert, by placing a piece on their tongue. The stone was also used for many diseases in olden days, by both internal and external application. Thus it would be exposed to sunlight and then laid on an unhealthy skin. Rock crystals were also used to stanch bleeding and stop diarrhoea, to cure giddiness and to help nursing mothers make milk. They were being sold by apothecaries as late as 1750 on the

Continent. When a disease was incurable the power of the crystal would be used up and it would disappear. Water in which a rock crystal has stood was thought to have curative properties. The Celtic St Columba presented a consecrated rock crystal to King Brude as a cure for his druid.

Generally speaking it can be said that rock crystal, which always expresses itself in triangles, contains and attracts the power of the light ether, and that the individual who has a specimen with him has something that will help his intuitive insight to penetrate the darkness of ignorance. Rock crystal also helps one to overcome anxiety (with symptoms such as diarrhoea or flight), not by letting everything take its course but by concentrating on the job in hand.

Rock crystal is taken to be a stone of the *Sun* and *Leo*, mainly because it is colourless like the diamond (the Rhinestone is nothing more than a coloured form of rock crystal).

Rock crystal has a positive and a negative pole. It *orientates* rather than leads; it concentrates the attention and points the spirit to God.

Agate

Agate is a stone of frequent occurrence which consists of silicon oxide. It is opaque and patterned and often displays irregular but concentric layers of material. Various terms are used to describe forms in which it occurs—terms such as clouded agate, fortification agate, moss agate and so on; moss agate (or dendritic agate) being a chalcedony properly speaking. The patternings are caused by gas bubbles in the liquid magma which leave spaces for coloured fluid silicon compounds to fill during fresh volcanic eruptions. Other elements are also free to enter these gaps, elements which include oxydizable iron, and traces of rarer metals, all of which combine to give the different colourations.

Agates are very plentiful in the town of Idar-Oberstein on the Nahe in Western Germany (Hunsrück) and here the traveller to the Stein-kaulenberg, a low afforested mountain ridge, can still see more than twenty caves where agates and amethysts used to be mined and where the occasional prospector still tries his luck. The business of the town is mainly concerned with cutting and polishing precious stones, and in small workshops and museums visitors can see highly polished cross-sections of enormous blocks of agate. Their colours usually range through reddish, brown, orange, yellow ochre, grey and liver-brown (any blue or green specimens having been artificially coloured). All kinds of ornaments and household articles are made of this material—for instance, knife-handles and the tops of bottle stoppers, and small dishes on which drugs were once rubbed down that are now used as ash-trays.

The so-called *moss agate* and *tree agate* (dendritic agate) do not have fossils embedded in them, as might be supposed; the tree-like formations are caused mainly by the manganese ore, pyrolusite, incorporated in the stone.

In ancient times, agate was worn to placate the gods. It was thought to protect the wearer to such an extent that Orpheus took it with him during his descent to Hades. Agate strengthens the heart, gives courage and is an antidote to poisons. It belongs to the tribe of Naphtali, a name which appropriately enough means 'my wrestling'. Remember, each of the twelve tribes of Israel had its own stone in the high priest's breastplate. It was considered easier to find an agate to wear for courage than to pluck a hair from a lion's mane for the same purpose. Agate, then, can be associated with Leo the lion; however, not every type of agate belongs to Leo. The striped sardonyx of the tribe of Ephraim does in fact do so but, on the basis of its colour, yellow agate is reckoned to be a stone of Gemini and Virgo.

Agate is said to reduce the temperature in fevers and even to have the ability of cooling water. It sharpens the sight, illuminates the mind, bestows eloquence, assists in the discovery of treasures and attracts inheritances (Scorpio). The powder was taken in apple juice as a remedy for insanity. Pliny reported that burning a piece of agate can avert tempests. Wearing moss agate improves the vitality.

Agate is a semi-precious stone; it does not permit the passage of light and so is one of the psychic, human stones, not one of the spiritual (transparent) stones.

It keeps the wearer from licentiousness and makes him serious and well-balanced (the onyx, being more saturnine, does this even more strongly).

In many countries the agate stands in high esteem. There is a small river in Sicily that used to be called the Agates, where people went fishing for the stones. St Agatha was the patron saint of Catania in Sicily and of Malta.

Agate amulets against snake-bite, paralysis and mental illness are worn in the Gold Coast (Ghana), and in Ancient Greece and Rome similar agate amulets were engraved with a dog's head and a lion and were worn against epilepsy and the plague. In Mexico agate dog's heads were given to the dead to make them strong and wakeful. An Anglo-Saxon manuscript of the tenth century recommends the taking of finely-powdered agate for possession by the Evil One and against assaults. Agate was also recommended for lightning stroke and scorpion stings, for bringing rain and for promoting childbirth and making it easier. The red-yellow or lion agate was very popular with the Roman gladiators. It was said to make a person loved and lovable.

Taking everything into consideration, we may conclude that agate strengthens the power of the *Sun* in its wearer, improving his ego and his self-esteem. Hence, too, it builds up resistance against the temptations of Scorpio (square to the Sign of Leo), such as sexual desire, emotionalism and the firing of the imagination. So it is good for those with the Sun in Scorpio or with an adverse Scorpio.

Carnelian

Carnelian (the name means 'flesh-coloured') is the stone the Bible translators call sardius or sard. Its colour ranges through white, light pink, flesh colour, orange, red, reddish brown and dark brown, and it was the dark brown variety that was called sard.

According to some translations, the sardius was the first stone in the breastplate of the Hebrew high priest. Now in my opinion it is the stone of purity of Virgo, the Virgin, and thus also that of pure blood, of racial purity. Racial purity was very important to the Children of Israel of course and we read in the Old Testament of how they were constantly warned against intermarriage with other peoples. A nation that becomes a people of mixed ancestry always becomes indifferent to and disloyal to its national spirit and religion.

It is not surprising therefore that the stone is also that of family unity, of the love of relatives for one another and of *blood ties*. Nowhere is this characteristic so strongly expressed as in Israel. For instance, there were Jewish children in the Second World War who were reared and educated by Christians, sometimes even being confined to Roman Catholic cloisters in ignorance of the Jewish Faith and without contact with their compatriots, and yet when they grew up they found work with Jewish employers and married Jewish partners. Whoever wishes to strengthen this characteristic should wear a carnelian. The fact that it has so often been used in signet rings is due not simply to its hardness but to its appropriateness, as an expression of racial integrity, for bearing the impression of a family coat of arms.

Talismans made from it protect the wearer from accidents, tempests and lightning, nightmares and the evil eye (in which case it is really an amulet). It stanches the flow of blood, antidotes infection and blood-poisoning by its cleansing power, soothes fevers, an overheated imagination and anger, and heals open sores.

The orange carnelian, belonging to Taurus, strengthens the voice, and makes a person both eloquent and charitable. It is also recommended for saturnine complaints such as melancholia, rheumatism and neuralgia.

The genuine dark sard comes from India and is said to be an Aries stone, although it seems to us to be more in keeping with Capricorn and thus to be suitable for saturnine diseases.

The dark red carnelians are usually the products of heating and of treatment with iron sulphate. This is what is done in Idar-Oberstein. These German stones are of South American origin (Brazil, Uruguay). The Indian and Chinese carnelians are paler. Especially fine statuettes are cut from the stone in China, use being made of the various tints in the stone.

Greek women used to wear a carnelian as part of their coiffures, perhaps as an aid to chastity. Carnelian is also connected with the sense of taste.

Onyx

Onyx is a variety of agate. Black onyx coloured black artificially has been produced for 5000 years. It is also called *nagel stone* or *nail* stone. Apparently it is good for the nails, hair and skin, for it is a stone of Saturn and Capricorn and belongs to the Apostle Philip. It is very suitable for cameos.

As a stone of Saturn it helps to settle karmic debts during the first thirty years of life. If the wearer has a strong and unafflicted Saturn in his or her horoscope, it brings seriousness, perseverance, humility, good morals, deep thoughts and spiritual strength, the holding in check of one's passions, tranquillity, reserve and fearlessness. It is good for watery eyes, suppuration, heart weakness, circulatory disorders and accidents.

When Saturn is badly placed in the horoscope, he can give harshness, dejection, unpleasant dreams and poverty and is liable to separate friends and marriage partners from one another. Onyxes are used in rosaries to aid thought concentration; they are also employed in signet rings and on articles of clothing worn during mourning.

The onyx helps hearing and listening. It is given in high homoeopathic potencies for certain ear diseases, and it is said to be the stone which lets one listen to God's voice, which is always speaking in our *conscience* and sometimes by way of *inspiration*. The onyx with a white circle in it is called the *lynx onyx*; the one with white stripes is known as *sardonyx*.

The *sardonyx* is reddish brown and is overlaid with white chalcedony or sard (= sardius); the two different coloured layers are used to advantage in cutting cameos or intaglios. It makes the wearer pleasant, gives self-control and happiness in marriage, attracts friends and gives success in matters involving the law. It is good for bites, infections, pain and poisoning.

Chalcedony

Chalcedony is a so-called cryptocrystalline variety of silicon dioxide, that is to say it has the same crystalline structure as rock crystal, but the details are identifiable only by means of a microscope or by X-ray analysis. Chalcedony with a coarse, long-grained structure absorbs no colouration and is therefore known as transparent or translucent white chalcedony, the genuine 'milk-stone' which, by the doctrine of signatures, has always been regarded as a means of inducing lactation in nursing mothers, a purpose for which it is still employed in Italy. When the grain is short, colouring matter is sometimes absorbed—in particular iron oxide and iron hydroxide—in which case the stone is no longer transparent and is called *jasper*. Dark green jasper with red flecks is known as heliotrope or bloodstone.

Chalcedony that is flesh-coloured is called *carnelian* or *cornelian*. The yellow variety is known as *canary stone*, the reddish brown as *sard* and the apple green as *chrysoprase*. There is also a blue chalcedony. When it has coloured bands in it, it is called *agate*. With inclusions, the latter becomes dendritic or moss agate, or enhydros (water enclosed in a thin envelope of chalcedony).

Chalcedony is made into beads, pendants and brooches and, for scientific purposes, into the cushions for the knives of fine balances.

White chalcedony is a so-called mother stone, which wraps up other types of rock in a covering of silicic acid or covers them like a scab does a healing wound. It also fills cavities. Sometimes it is found within amethyst crystals like a light in the darkness. This maternalism is strongly reminiscent of Cancer and the Moon, to which we must certainly assign white chalcedony, the *pietra latte* or milkstone (a term also applied to white agate and white serpentine). The suggestion of binding up and healing is seen in the fact that chalcedony joins together layers of agate and heals the wounds of broken stones. In Tibet, chalcedony was seen as the image of the pure lotus flower, a half-transparent white. Chalcedony is also deliberately tinted with metal salts.

Yellow, lilac, pink, light blue, grey and white are the most suitable colours for women and promote maternal feelings. The darker shades are more suitable for men and give resignation. In everyone, chalcedony increases goodwill, reduces touchiness and turns the thoughts inwards.

When in contact with morbid skin excretions, chalcedony loses its colour. It is a styptic for wounds, absorbs poisons and protects against hypnosis.

Chrysoprase

Chrysoprase is an apple-green chalcedony containing a fair number of white streaks and flaws. The green colour, which is due to nickel, tends to fade after a period of exposure to light. The cause is loss of water and the original tint can sometimes be restored by burying the stone in damp earth or by laying it in a nickel sulphate solution. The heat generated by polishing will often produce small cracks in the stone and therefore it is not a favourite stone with which to work. However it has been used for mosaics and inlaid work since the fourteenth century.

The stone was found in Silesia where it is popular for helping confinements. After the mines had been abandoned for a long time, the stone was rediscovered in 1740 by a Prussian officer in the mill of Kosemütz. Frederick the Great took an interest in the stone and had two tables with tops made of chrysoprase brought into his palace of Sans Souci.

Besides being found in the region to the south of Breslau, chrysoprase is mined in the Urals, Brazil, California, Arizona and Oregon, often in association with opal and colourless chalcedony.

The chrysoprase sold in the trade is often nothing more than chalcedony that has been stained green. The green tint, which has been obtained artificially by soaking in a nickel or chromium salt solution followed by heating, later fades away or is replaced by a brown colour or becomes cloudy. Always insist on 'natural chrysoprase'.

The Romans called chrysoprase a stone of Venus, but it frequently exerts a strong Lunar influence. Chrysoprase helps to make conscious what was unconscious, strengthens the workings of insight and the higher consciousness, encourages hope and improves the eyesight. It clarifies problems, due mainly to the transparent quality of the stone. Anyone who wishes to use it for the eyes should do so preferably when the Moon is in Taurus or Cancer.

In the Middle Ages, it was prized as a cure for restlessness, for making the wearer quick-witted and for imparting adaptability and presence of mind. It was carried as a protection by those undertaking sea-voyages. There seems to be something of Mercury in all this.

Amethyst

Amethyst occurs both in non-crystalline and crystalline forms, but always in a light or dark purple. It is an ancient precious stone in the sense that it made its appearance when the stones of the Earth's crust were still hardly solid. Gem colours are produced by traces of the metals iron, manganese and titanium among others, as we find in the amethyst, sapphire and rose quartz. If rose quartz crystals are heated, the dark colour of the titanium disappears and when it has cooled down the crystals remain colourless. But when sapphire is heated, the blue of the titanium is retained, since the colour is stronger and more full of life in the older stone. In the youngest stones, titanium is found only in *acicular rutile*, the so-called Venus' hair stone or *flèches d'amour*, in which needles of titanium oxide are embedded in quartz.

In amethyst it is interesting that the purple colour due to manganese is strongest at the top of the crystal. The tiny columns of the crystals are but little developed and only their tops are seen clustered together. At least, this is true of the smaller specimens deposited in a so-called *druse*, a mother stone of chalcedony or agate. Sometimes, if a plain black porphyry or piece of agate is split open, a cluster of amethyst crystals can be seen inside. Each crystal is built up in layers and thus points to a rhythmic development reminiscent of the vegetable kingdom. Many pieces of agate with amethysts inside them used to be found in Idar-Oberstein, but now they mainly come from Brazil and Uruguay; however, those with the lightest colour and the most beautiful glitter come from the Urals. These rocks can be a metre long and oval in shape; in Brazil one was discovered 10 metres long and 5 metres high and containing 700 tons of first-sized amethysts.

The very dark purple *Jacobin* comes from South West Africa; its colour is produced by iron thiocyanate and manganese, although in the very light-coloured stones from Bolivia titanium is present and this causes the formation of a slimmer crystal structure, for titanium is upward-striving (like the Titans who strove to break free from the underworld). In our day and age titanium is being used in space rockets.

It is through its titanium content, therefore, that amethyst is the stone of *absolute power* and is set in the bishop's ring as it was in the rings of German kings and dukes. The king's herald showed this ring when he summoned the vassals to war. Amethyst bestows the favour of those in high places.

The amethyst's manganese content gives the power of *creative thinking*, which is why this stone is much used in meditation and in general for *spiritual cleansing and development*. The colour violet is serious in tone and forms the Bridge over Nothing* connecting earth with heaven. The amethyst belongs to the Sign of Pisces, the Fish, and is found in the Pope's Fisherman's Ring. It is also a protection against drunkenness (a-methyl = anti-alcohol), the failing of Pisces; for that purpose it is worn in the navel. It counteracts the absent-mindedness of Pisces, gives clarity in prophesy and the interpretation of dreams, plus humility, philanthropy and friendship (it is given to a friend, but if the friend gets rid of it the friendship is broken).

Amethyst helps to get *right* on the side of its wearer; in China, for instance, amethysts were rented to individuals engaged in lawsuits. What is more, amethyst helps fishermen make catches (Pisces) and encourages the growth of plants below ground. For insomnia, an amethyst is used to stroke the temples. It affords protection against blood diseases, venereal diseases and puerperal fever, also hysteria, neuralgia, hallucinations, fits, hatred and rage, fear, grief and homesickness.

Amethyst cures impurities of the skin. The procedure is to place the stone in a pot of boiling water and to wash the skin with the drops formed in the lid. It is also employed in cases of dropsy and colour blindness.

The amethyst is the stone of St Valentine and gives happiness in marriage if the wife gives her husband one set in a silver heart.

---

*The Rainbow Bridge. *Translator's note.*

If anyone has an amethyst in prison, they will feel as if they were in the open air. What I mean by this is that the amethyst raises the spirit to the realms of infinity and that even if an individual is sitting within the confinement of walls in his physical body, he will sense that he is surrounded by the measureless universe. In the Middle Ages amethyst was more expensive than diamond, and even though the value of the amethyst has been brought down following the discovery of the rich deposits of gems in South America, it is still reckoned among the most precious of precious stones. It has no fire but certainly scintillates. As men began to take less interest in spiritual things, the amethyst was devalued. At the end of the eighteenth century, Queen Charlotte possessed an amethyst necklace valued at two thousand pounds which would now fetch no more than half that amount.

In Greenland blue amethysts are used as a shiny top dressing for gravel paths—a clear indication of the way in which the spiritual aspirations of the Middle Ages have been downgraded in the search for physical comfort.

Aventurine

Aventurine is a faintly translucent type of quartz spangled with inclusions of minerals which determine its colour and give it a certain glitter. Thus mica makes it silvery or coppery, chrome mica makes it green and haematite makes it red to brown. (An imitation of the brown variety is the so-called *gold-stone*, which used to be made into cigar-holders. It is a sort of glass, that is melted for small flakes of copper to be stirred in.)

The reddish brown sort comes from Siberia and Madagascar, and bestows vitality.

The green sort comes from India and Nepal. It marks a combination of the Moon and Uranus and gives unexpected and surprising adventures and luck in love and games. It makes an individual independent and original. Green aventurine has a binding and healing force and is good for skin diseases (Libra). The imperial seal of China was cut from aventurine (at a time before jade became popular there) because the stones of heaven were all thought to be green.

A blue variety, *vivianite*, contains iron phosphate and comes from Brazil and Madagascar.

Opal

Opal varies in colour from milky white to greenish yellow and brick red. It is slightly translucent and has a glassy, almost greasy sheen. Consisting of colloidal silica, it holds a large amount of water and also some air; hence it is supposed to exert a curative action on the lungs. The water content is from 6 to 34 per cent. Being iridescent with all the colours of the rainbow, it reflects totality, in a manner of speaking. In dry air it loses moisture and the play of colour, but after spending a while in damp air once more, both are regained. Neptune and the Moon govern this stone.

The shifting colours, producers of opalescence, arise through the reflection and refraction of light at different intensities by the water and the minute cracks in the stone. They are called interference colours. There is something alluring and seductive about the opal and it stimulates the wearer's erotic and emotional nature and his or her thirst for life. Since most of us develop the influence of Neptune on a low level, the opal often leads to frivolous adventures. The stone's range of colours accommodates all possible sins, but when a person is bent on enjoying Neptunian sensations, he must blame not the stone but himself for any misfortunes: the stone does no more than activate his inclinations.

Because it is considered unlucky, it may not be worn at court in England or Sweden, and the Spanish royal family actually owned an unlucky opal. When Alphonso XII married Princess Mercedes, the Countess of Castiglione, his discarded sweetheart, presented him with a valuable opal ring as a memento of their former association. The young queen, Mercedes, was so fascinated by its beauty that she begged him to let her wear it. Within a few months, she died of a mysterious disease. Then the ring was worn by the king's grandmother, who thereupon quickly passed away. The king gave the ring to his sister, the Infanta Maria, who died of the same inexplicable illness. Anyone would think that by this time he would have realized something was wrong, but not a bit of it: the king now decided to wear the ring himself and died of the very same disease in an equally short space of time. After that, Queen Christine let the ring hang on a golden chain around the image of the patron saint of Madrid, the Holy Lady of Alumdena.

According to the occultist Laarss, no one ought to wear an opal who has Saturn afflicted in his or her horoscope, but it can do no harm with the Sun in Libra and Venus and Saturn in good aspect to one another. However, it must not be used for selfish ends.

In Greece it is believed that the opal carries the spirit of truth in it and reveals the future to its owner. It is said to turn dull when bad luck is on the way. This, of course, is the higher working of Neptune.

Geologically, opal can be regarded as a young stone, still in the jelly stage; as an embryo snatched from the warm moist womb of mother earth, it must be cherished until it has grown accustomed to the external world.

One variety is the Mexican *hydrophane* which, rather exceptionally, displays beautiful colours when dry but is clear and colourless when placed in water. It is so porous that it can stick to the tongue, and air plays a more important part in it than water does. The hydrophane has been called the World Eye on account of its near transparency and is thought to exert a healing power on the eyes. It is found in Hubertusberg in Saxony among other places.

White opals should be viewed in full daylight, as they often look more beautiful than they really are—again a Neptunian trait.

Fire opal is not an opal that has more 'fire' than other opals, it gets its name from its orange-flame colour. Opal can form a soft shell over wood and even over the bones of prehistoric animals, as in Australia for example. Shells, sponges, fish bones and the stems of plants are also found opalised.

A notable example is the *Tabashir* or *bamboo opal*, found in the lowermost sections of bamboo stems in Burma. It is due to the large amounts of silica which the bamboo takes up out of the water. This opal looks more like a pearl and is regarded as very holy.

Another interesting phenomenon is the opal found as an excretion of silicic acid in the brain of the Kubi fish in Japan; it is white and lustreless.

Geyserite (or *sinter*) occurs as a sort of natural kettle-fur near the silica-rich water of the geysers of Iceland, Turkey and Yellowstone Park in the USA.

Rose Quartz

Rose quartz is rock crystal that has been coloured by manganese. It is crystalline, but only one example of a rose quartz crystal with regularly bounded flat surfaces exists, and that is found in the Museum for Natural History in Boston, USA. The colour is often unevenly distributed through the material, which has rather a lot of small cracks in it. It is made into beads, small vases, ash-trays and paper weights, also pendants and cabochons for brooches and rings. Sometimes they contain asterisms or light-stars. These are due to inclusions of extremely minute rutile crystals and the star usually has six rays. The pink shade is delicate and can be bleached by sunlight.

Rose quartz occurs as an intergrowth in granite (pegmatite). A rare transparent variety called *Rosaline* is found in Madagascar. Rose quartz is a mollifying, sweet and gentle stone of Venus. It is suitable for young girls, artists and insipid young men, who are very fond of it. It makes a person receptive to beauty, to colours and sounds, to sculpture, painting, music and poetry. It enlivens the imagination to enable it to create beautiful forms. It also opens the eyes to physical beauty and makes a person loved—or doted on. It accords well with the 15th degree of Virgo, i.e. the section between 14 and 15.

Citrine

Citrine is a yellow quartz, often called *gold topaz* in the trade; however, it is much cheaper than real topaz. Citrine is a rock crystal containing iron, and it is obvious that at some stage it must have been exposed to very high temperatures (over 800 degrees Centigrade) in order for the yellow colour to have been produced. The majority of citrines are found in Ceylon and in the gravel beds of Brazil. When the output began to become exhausted, man started to imitate nature by heating amethysts into citrines or topaz-brûlé. It had been observed that in forest fires amethysts buried out of the reach of air in layers of clay became yellow or yellow brown when exposed to the heat, and the process was copied artificially. Yellow or orange-red citrines are produced in this manner. Small streaks can often be seen in these heat-treated amethysts when they are viewed in transmitted light. Lovely natural citrines used to come from the Gotthard region, but now they are very rare.

Gold topaz, Madeira topaz, Palmyra or *Bahia topaz* are nothing but citrine, in other words quartz. The whiskey-coloured *Scots topaz* or Cairngorm lies between the citrine and the *smoky quartz* (also known as smoky topaz).

It may be gathered from the many intrigues associated with it that the citrine is ruled by Mercury. It inclines the wearer to adopt a neutral attitude and gives him a sensible control over his emotional life. It makes the mood a sunny and cheerful one, makes the thoughts clear and animates the circulation of the blood and of electricity through the nerves. It belongs, quite suitably to the Sign of Gemini.

Plasma

Plasma is a leek-green stone, often speckled white, sometimes flecked with yellow. It is an opaque stone and its green colour is caused by inclusions of green delessite. Apart from its colour it is the same as bloodstone.

Prase is very similar but is translucent and sometimes occurs as crystals. The raw material is found in the east of India and in Germany.

Praseolite

This is a transparent green quartz from Mexico and Brazil which is polished in Rio de Janeiro. It is slightly radioactive. By heating it, different shades of green are produced. Some specimens look like green beryl, others like peridot or green tourmaline. Artificial ones are manufactured by irradiating amethysts in a cyclotron.

The way in which heating imparts a green colour to amethyst was discovered by a dealer in minerals in California who was carrying a stock of amethysts from Arizona. His store was destroyed in a fire and he found that the colour of his amethysts had been changed by the heat into various shades of apple green. Subsequently, systematic tests were carried out to discover what temperatures and what heating times would give the desired results.

Jasper

Jasper is really a very common and insignificant stone, freely occurring in our garden gravel. It is dull, compact and solid and contains iron oxides and silicates, whence its red, brown, yellow, green or grey colouration. The red-brown variety is also known as *silex*.

An imitation lapis lazuli is made from it with Berlin blue and is called *Swiss lapis*, but the blue quickly fades.

Jasper is found in Ontario, the USA, Germany, Russia and Sicily in mountainous regions. There is a hill at Chkalov in Russia consisting entirely of pale green and dark red jasper.

Jasper was greatly prized in antiquity, and engraved ring stones of it have been found in Pompei and Herculaneum and many other old cities. Powerful magical and healing properties have always been ascribed to it, and in all ages it has been worn in the navel for stomach ache. Sometimes it has been worn as an amulet in the form of a serpent emitting rays (as for instance by King Nechepsos of Egypt in 900 B.C.), apparently indicating that the stone itself emits life force. It was also recommended for all wasting diseases.

People have always looked on it as a stone of Virgo, Libra and Scorpio. A scorpion was engraved in it while the Sun was in Scorpio and it was then worn for stone in the bladder. Such talismans are still worn in England.

Jasper improves the sense of smell and therefore can be worn to cure loss of smell. This has to do with the liver and, in Iran, powdered jasper is given with powdered turquoise for diseases of the gall bladder, liver and kidneys. The gall and liver belong to Virgo and the kidneys to Libra.

Jasper also has some connection with the start of pregnancy and helps against the vomiting which often occurs at that time. This is especially true of the jasper agate. In English-speaking countries the remedy for the condition just mentioned and for epilepsy is a medicine made of finely powdered jasper, coral and Nux vomica.

Red jasper was greatly venerated in ancient Peru.

A high value was also set on it in the Bible. It is the stone of un-selfishness and is known as the mother of all stones. In some versions it is the last stone in the high priest's breastplate. Beginning with sardius and ending with jasper, we have the development from Aries to Pisces, with the love of one's blood relatives giving place in the end to the general love of all mankind.

Green jasper was an especial favourite in the mystical Christendom of the Middle Ages, and so too was the green stone flecked with red jasper that is known as *bloodstone* or *heliotrope*. Green, said the mystic Jan van Ruysbroek, is the colour of the plants, and plants lift themselves towards the sunlight; therefore, a green stone helps the human soul to strive upwards towards the light of the spirit. It strengthens the will to do good and to offer oneself as an instrument of the divine Spirit.

In the New Testament, the twelve stones are named again, but there the first is jasper and the last is amethyst. These are the stones of the New Jerusalem, or of spiritualized man, and for the attainment of spirituality one must definitely *begin* with *good will*.

Silex (Hornstone)

Silex is an impure form of flint which is sometimes passed off as jasper. It is reddish, brown or yellow and contains iron. In earlier days it was used for striking fire and also for warding off unwanted fire such as the lightning stroke. 'Thunderbolts' made from it long ago can still be found in the Dutch countryside. Stone Age cultures made tools and weapons from it, and in S.W. Africa, the Nilotic region and in the Indre Department of France, silex jewellery has been found.

Heliotrope

Heliotrope is a green chalcedony with red flecks of jasper. It is said to reflect sunlight with a blood-red glow. In Christian symbolism, stories have been woven around it, such as that the red flecks are drops of blood from Jesus on the cross. These flecks contain iron, which is styptic; therefore the stone is dipped in cold water and used on wounds. Those who wear the stone are said to be protected against wounds, scorpion bites, vermin and poison. It is supposed to stop nose-bleeds, to cure piles (haemorrhoids) and, when worn over the solar plexus it is said to strengthen the stomach and intestines and to remove stone in the bladder.

As a stone of Virgo, it is good for agriculture and horticulture; it enables crops and animals to flourish and wards off hail and drought.

It has been claimed that the heliotrope phosphoresces and that one could even light the candles on the altar with it. When inherited, it gives the wearer the help and support of the one to whom it once belonged. It gives glimpses of the past and future and, when the waxing moon is near the earth, it brings prophetic dreams.

Heliotrope allegedly bestows invisibility and wisdom, idealism and fellow-feeling and, in general, unselfishness.

The stone is set in silver and gold and is made into seals and cameos. When polished it has a beautiful shine.

The ancient Greeks and Romans employed the heliotrope for an easy confinement in women.

It is sometimes called the stone of St Joseph.

Smoky Quartz

The reddish brown variety of quartz, containing iron, titanium or carbon, is named smoky quartz. The lightest kind is the so-called *smoky topaz* or *Cairngorm* of Scotland; the darkest is the dark-brown *morion*, verging on black, found in Dauphiné, where it is worn as a half-mourning or deep-mourning stone.

On being heated, smoky quartz loses its brown colour and turns into rock crystal, so to speak. Russian peasants achieve this transformation by baking smoky quartz in their bread.

The stone belongs to Saturn and its Sign Capricorn, the Sea-goat, and to serious, solid, thrifty and suspicious folk. It binds its wearer to the earth and so makes a good talisman for soldiers in time of war. However, it can also make the wearer gloomy.

Cat's Eye, Hawk's Eye and Tiger's Eye

Cat's eye, hawk's eye and tiger's eye are fibrous quartzes mingled with vessels of hornblende-asbestos. The *cat's eye* contains olive-green asbestos, the *hawk's eye* (due to phosphorus) blue-green and the *tiger's eye* golden pigments. The *tiger's eye* is formed from the *hawk's eye* by the oxidation of the iron in it. If these stones are cut in a rounded shape (as cabochons), a silky shine is created which appears to move about with shifts in the incident light (iridescence) and makes the stone look lifelike. These stones certainly resemble eyes and it should come as no surprise that they have been worn down the ages to avert the evil eye and to cure eye diseases. They help people to gain insight into their own faults and to perceive and think more clearly, with the sharp eye of the beast of prey (circumspection is implied too).

The quartz *cat's eye* is to be found in the Bavarian town of Hof. These magnesium-containing eye-stones are worn for enterospasm and asthma.

The chrysoberyl *cat's eye* or *cymophane* is much more expensive than the *quartz cat's eye*. Cat's eyes of all sorts have always made a deep impression on mankind. There are even individuals who shudder just on looking at them. No wonder people in the East ascribed a demonic power to the cat's eye, a power strong enough to keep lesser demons under control. When Victoria was Queen of England, the conquered Indian King of Candy had to permit an enormous cat's eye of about 313 carats to leave his treasure chamber for presentation to the British Queen. Its demon was then able to look after the Empire.

As soon as a beautiful cat's eye is discovered, the East Asian market snaps it up. It is difficult to bring such specimens to the West.

Rutile

Rutile is clear rock crystal in which golden or reddish hairlike needles of titanium are present (the so-called Venus' hair).

In present-day France, necklaces of rutile are recommended for bronchitis by doctors. Obviously it is a stone that is very appropriate to Gemini.

The translucent red stone with the metallic sheen is especially pretty. There are also dark brown and black specimens (*nigrine*). The crystals are found in the USA, Brazil, France and Norway. The ore was formerly used as a black pigment for decorating porcelain and for tinting glass purple. It is now manufactured synthetically as well. As titanium white it provides a good but expensive paint. Since the natural crystals are much less suitable than the synthetic ones for fashioning as gems, artificial rutile is in great demand. The light blue variety is marketed as *Titania Night Stone*, which sparkles even more brilliantly than diamond and has a colour-play reminiscent of the opal. It is made up into pendants and brooches but is too soft for ring-stones.

Rhinestone

This stone, related to the opal, is really a rock crystal with small cracks producing interference colours. Since these cracks sometimes contain water or carbonic acid solution, cutting them is rather risky for, if the cracks are laid open, the liquid will run away and the shimmering rainbow effect will disappear. Therefore, genuine cut Rhinestones are quite expensive and what the tourists buy in the gift shops along the Rhine and Moselle are worthless imitations.

Obsidian

Obsidian is lava from a volcanic eruption, lava that has solidified so quickly that no crystals can be formed in it. It is volcanic glass or fused quartz. It consists mainly of silica, aluminium and sometimes of a certain amount of potassium, sodium and iron oxide. It has a glassy surface and is fairly fragile.

Obsidian is found along the English coast, in Hungary and Siberia and in Mexico, Oregon and Nevada.

It was popular with the preconquest Indian population of America since a very sharp edge can be imparted to knives, spearheads and arrowheads made from it. The Spanish invaders had a healthy respect for the Aztec itzli. Vases and mirrors of obsidian have frequently been recovered from ancient Mexican graves, and arrowheads and needles of this material have been found in the old obsidian mines of Oregon. It also decorated the festal attire of the White Deer Skin tribe during their biennial song and dance ceremonies.

Blue obsidian is found on the coast of Britain and is cut into beautiful translucent pendants. Darker, brown and black varieties, which are sometimes flecked with white, are obtained from the Italian Lipari Islands, from Iceland and from the USA. The white flecks of so-called christobalite are formed at temperatures of more than 2500°C. Sometimes bergmahonie, a brown obsidian with red flame markings, is found. Obsidian is said to sharpen both the external and the internal vision.

Tektite (Moldavite)
Tektite is a quartz glass derived from meteorites. Tektites are found as spherical or oval pieces etched with grooves. Translucent dark green tektites come from Moldavia in Czechoslovakia and from Indo China, while other green varieties occur in Australia and the Philippines. A black form found in the tin-lodes on the islands of Banka and Billiton is made into love charms. The Cathars in the Pyrenees, who took refuge from their persecutors in the caves there, used to wear these small black stones from the skies, keeping them in small bags next to their skin.

Moldavite is a transparent bottle-green and the colour shows up well when the stone is polished. There often seem to be small bubbles trapped inside it. Moldavite is sometimes sold under the name of water-chrysolite or bottle-stone.

Similar tektites have been found in the Libyan desert, south-west of Cairo. Pieces of 3kg and heavier were discovered in pits between the sand dunes. A 52-carat specimen is on display in the British Museum.

These tektites are also encountered in the enormous crater in Siberia made by a gigantic meteor in June 1980 or, as has been suggested, by a UFO which went out of control and plunged to destruction at that time. Herdsmen and cattle were killed over a very wide area and many displayed symptoms of radio-active poisoning.

Now, it is an interesting but puzzling fact, that similar fused products have also been found after atomic testing in Nevada and after atomic bombs were dropped on Hiroshima and Nagasaki. It is striking that, in the Nevada desert where tests are now carried out, brown tektites known as Apache tears (probably because they are practically transparent) are already present.

17.

BERYLS

Alexandrite
Emerald
Aquamarine

Spectacles are called *Brille* in German, *bril* in Dutch, because lenses used to be cut and polished from the *beryl*. All the varieties of beryl contain the metal beryllium, which is even lighter than aluminium, with which it is bound in silicic acid and pipe-clay. It comes in hexagonal crystals. The usual green beryl is green or yellow and contains iron. Sometimes there is a red glow in the green, and clair-voyants read meanings into it. It protects sailors and adventurers. It has a good effect on the mouth, jaw, throat, stomach and liver.

Morganite, named after the collector Morgan, is pink due to its iron and manganese content. It also contains nickel, copper and the alkaline element caesium.

Golden beryl contains uranium.

Heliodor is greenish-gold.

The *Euclase* has transparent blue-green prismatic crystals of elegant appearance much sought after by collectors. Unfortunately it splits so easily that it is unsuitable for wearing in rings. The sea-green tint, reminiscent of aquamarine, indicates that this beryl is a stone of Neptune.

The *Phenakite* is bluish-yellow, pink or colourless and used to be mistaken for rock crystal (appropriately enough, the name is derived from a Greek word meaning deceiver), but it is much harder. It has the same glassy sheen as quartz and emerald.

The *chrysoberyl* does not contain silica but is surprisingly hard. Its green colour is due to chromium. It also contains aluminium.

The *chrysoberyl cat's eye* or *cymophane* has a silky sheen like a cat's eye, the yellow-green sort has more sun power, the green sort more moon power. This stone, which must be visible when it is worn, is held in high esteem in India, where it is said to give gain and prosperity, gambler's luck, far-sightedness and financial ability. It helps the mental balance and drives away night terrors, asthma and croup. The greener specimens are more suited to Taurus, the yellower ones are more suited to Gemini. The beryls crystallize in hexagonal prisms with pyramidal ends or, more usually with one pyramidal end. Sometimes these six-sided columns are simply enormous, but then they are too impure to use as gemstones. In Maine (USA) a crystal of beryl 6m long has been found, and in Ponferrada, Leon, Spain, these large beryl pillars are used as door-posts.

The beryls, especially those that are blue and green, are Neptunian stones which sharpen the inner and the outer sight. They keep the brain active (Mercury-Neptune), uncover what is concealed and make a person sensitive to human radiations. They promote telepathy. They are given to the bride so that her aura and that of her bridegroom will unite satisfactorily with one another.

Alexandrite

This is a dark green variety of chrysoberyl which looks red by transmitted light, especially by candlelight or paraffin lamplight. It was first found in the Urals in 1830 on the birthday of the Czar, Alexander II, after whom it was called. Appropriately enough, red and green were the national colours of Russia. Now it is also found in Sri Lanka.

It is a stone which almost never contains impurities and is gloriously brilliant when cut. In order to take advantage of the colour change, the stone must be cut as a brilliant and the table must be very accurately orientated in order to obtain 'a green day and a red night'. This phenomenon also occurs in some sapphires. A story based on this fact and entitled *Le Saphire* [sic] *Merveilleux* was written by Mme de Genlis (1746-1830), in which the sapphire could indicate the unfaithfulness of a married woman within four hours. The one making the test had to ensure that the wife in question wore the sapphire during four hours of daylight.

Emerald

The emerald is a famous stone, celebrated in many a song, that has been found and prized ever since the Stone Age. In about 2500 B.C. it was already being extracted from the rocks of Upper Egypt. Cleopatra's gem mines, fifteen miles north of Asswan, were forgotten until they were rediscovered by Cailliand in 1818. However, they are no longer exploited, as the Egyptian emerald is pale and often cloudy and is therefore unable to compete with the much more beautiful South American stones, the best of which come from Columbia, with the somewhat paler kinds coming from Brazil. The latter are nevertheless preferred since they radiate much harmony and a great deal of light in spite of the fact they do not have such a pure, deep, radiant green as the stones from Columbia and Zimbabwe.

In India, too, emeralds are found, but the stones which bore this name in the past seem often to have been *peridots, green corundums* or *demantoids*. A demantoid can look remarkably like an emerald but experts tell them apart by their lustre, the emerald having the lustre of glass and the demantoid that of diamond. The Duke of Devonshire owns a magnificent Indian emerald crystal 5cm square weighing more than 1000 carats. It has many inclusions but a superb colour and, since it has never been cut, it is a museum piece.

The traditional way of treating an emerald was to do no more than cut it and set it in a golden claw so that it could sparkle from a crown, turban or throne as the shifting light fell on it from as many angles as possible. The great respect in which the stones were held usually overcame the temptation to satisfy personal vanity, but occasionally they were pierced and strung on necklaces.

The six-sided crystals of emerald are so large at times that they can be employed as pillars, and two such emerald pillars, nineteen to twenty feet high are known to have been standing in an Egyptian temple as late as A.D. 1650.

The ancient Romans and Phoenicians used to fetch emerald from Habach on the snow-line of the Taurus Mountains, and the Scythians found them in the Urals. Emeralds were also collected by the Etruscans.

When the Spanish invaders encountered the Aztecs of Mexico and the Incas of Peru, they discovered enormous quantities of emeralds in the royal treasure chambers and in the temples of these nations, some stones being the size of ostrich eggs. It was believed that they were indwelt by the goddess Esmeralda—obviously the power of the planet Venus which streamed out.

Pizarro, the ferocious Spanish conquistador, presented to Pope Clement VI a huge emerald he had stolen from the Incas, but he was not able to lay his hands on everything. In the temple of the sun at Cuzco there was an enormous emerald, the so-called emerald mother, on the altar; this and the famous neck-chain of the emperor Atahualpa, were hidden by courtiers in a cave. The chain of office contained fifty-two emeralds, each of them as big as a pigeon's egg and with a phase of the moon engraved on each one. These alternated with fifty-two large sapphires.

The ancient Greeks termed the emerald a stone of Venus; it also accords well with the Signs of Taurus and Libra. However, its green colour (probably due to chromium) also speaks of the Moon. Egyptian lying-in women used to wear an emerald engraved with a picture of Isis, the universal mother, in order to prevent miscarriages. Like many other green stones, it also suits Cancer. The early Christian church had Communion cups cut from it.

Traditionally, the emerald was said to protect against temptation and seduction; as a stone of Libra it preserved the marriage bond and if there was any unfaithfulness it became dull. The emerald keeps its wearer fresh and youthful and strengthens the sight (Nero used to look at the gladiators in the arena through an emerald!), which is why gem-cutters use it to refresh their tired eyes.

In addition, it strengthens the intellect and the memory, and helps to cure insomnia and bad dreams, not to speak of weakness, malaria, epilepsy and bleeding. It protects the wearer when he is travelling and makes him eloquent.

Because of the power radiating from them, emeralds worn in jewellery will catch the eye even in a large room occupied by many ladies adorned with other precious stones.

Aquamarine

Aquamarine means 'sea-water', and the blue-green colour of this stone is strongly reminiscent of the latter. It is completely transparent and, when cut, gives the wonderful light-effect of the sun on the waves, almost as if it were alive. It is the stone of pure-souled seers and mystics who feel everything. It is an expression of Uranus in or associated with air signs, and of clarity of mental vision and omniscience.

Since this stone is good for the eyes, spectacles used to be made from it. It is best worn in a long necklace so that it can hang down beside the heart and influence the solar plexus. The wearer is made youthful and fearless, has a true and warm heart, loves family and friends and enjoys a happy marriage. Innocence and purity are preserved by it. It helps against nerve pains, gland troubles, disorders of the neck, jaw and throat, against toothache, cough and stomach, liver and eye troubles. As might be expected, it safeguards mariners.

Like the turquoise it is a stone of Aquarius, but it seems to me that Neptune is at work in it in addition to Uranus; on this occasion in a beneficial way and at a high level. The crystals are hexagonal.

18.

CORUNDUMS

Corundum	Spinel
Ruby	Zircon
Sapphire	Jacinth
Padparadschah	Topaz

Corundum is a form of aluminium oxide, a primary mineral, occurring in some metamorphic calcareous sandstones and schists. Hexagonal crystals frequently occur in it; the red ones are called rubies and the blue ones are called sapphires. Corundum also occurs in the form of dark grains mixed with magnetite and is then known as emery, which is made into abrasive paper because it is so hard—with only one degree of hardness less than the diamond. There are colourless, yellow, yellow-green, blue-green, purple and pink corundums. In the trade, all those corundums which do not have a red shade are called *sapphires*. Green, purple and yellow corundums are known as *Oriental emerald*, *Oriental amethyst* and *Oriental topaz*. The pink variety is just known as corundum.

The forces of light act particularly strongly in the ruby and the sapphire, especially when they are *star stones*. Star stones contain extremely fine needles of other minerals which usually have little colour themselves. When the stone is moved the light strikes these needles at another angle and then a bright six-pointed star appears (asterism). Such stones are not cut with facets but as rounded, polished stones (*cabochons*).

Ruby and *sapphire* are mainly found in Burma, Thailand and Sri Lanka. The Burmese rubies are coloured the famous pigeon blood red. Around the city of Mogok in Burma the whole population over a small area is engaged in the finding of and trading in the gems that are found there.

The Ratnapoora district in Sri Lanka is an important source of sapphires, rubies, topazes, zircons, moonstones, tourmalines, etc. They are sold in the capital, Colombo, and many Dutchmen who used to travel to and from the Dutch East Indies in earlier times would buy their precious stones there. Often they found subsequently that they had been cheated, because synthetic stones were also imported in large quantities and sold by the Cingalese as genuine natural stones.

In the days when the Arabs, who did not understand the language of the Cingalese, came to make purchases in Ratnapoora, the still current method of negotiation was worked out, in which the seller and the buyer take each other's hand under a cloth. The prospective buyer will make his bid by counting the finger-joints of the merchant until he has reached the amount he has in mind. The merchant then makes his counter-offer in the same way. If agreement is reached, the seller squeezes the hand of the buyer. In this way bystanders are prevented from following the negotiations.

Many wonderful tales are told about how precious stones were obtained in Sri Lanka. There is a mountain there, 7352 feet high, known as Adams Peak. In the wet season the rivers pour down its sides with the stones they have washed out of the soil, and people down below have only to pick them up. In the dry season use is made of the fact that many eagles nest on top of the mountain. Pieces of meat are thrown down at the bottom of the mountain and the eagles swoop down on them and carry them away to their eyries. On the way, however, they are compelled to take a rest and stones stick to the flesh hanging from their beaks. As they continue their homeward flight, the lightly attached stones drop off and roll down the mountain. In the Thousand and One Nights, Sinbad the Sailor has an adventure in Ceylon, where he finds himself in the valley of diamonds, also occupied by huge serpents. When diamond hunters threw pieces of meat into the valley, he stuffed his bag full of diamonds and tied himself to one of the pieces of meat so that one of the eagles could pick him up with the meat and take him away from that dangerous place.

Ruby

The ruby is a corundum which crystallizes in the trigonal system. Its red colour is due to chromium oxide. The deepest red stones come from Burma, whereas those from Thailand incline to a brownish red owing to the presence of iron oxide. Those from Sri Lanka are raspberry red. The ruby often contains inclusions of rutile needles which give it a silky lustre. The name ruby comes from the Latin word *rubeus* meaning red.

Rubies are usually small, but the big ones are carat for carat more costly than diamonds. In the seventeenth century, the French buyer of precious stones, Tavernier, braved many dangers and hardships to go to India. He complained in his diary about how he had to travel in a flat boat up a river through a jungle full of lions, tigers and elephants (he gave rein to his fancy here, because there are no lions), before reaching the mines and when he arrived he found rubies of not more than four carats.

In India, the ruby is called the *Lord of all Stones*. Formerly, all precious stones that were as red as coral or yellow as saffron were the property of the rulers. Even the caste system was pressed into service to describe precious stones: the red ruby was a brahmin and male. The light sapphire was regarded as a brahmin too, but the darker sort was low caste and female. Cutting and polishing was managed in such a way as to bring out the beauty of the colour as much as might be; on the other hand, every effort was made to cut away as little of the stones as possible, since the rajahs counted their wealth in weight of precious stones.

Rubies are obtained from scree by ore-washing. It is not often that the fiery-red ruby crystals are found now in the white marble which is their mother-stone. At one time they were found in great plenty east of Kabul in Afghanistan, if the evidence is to be believed.

The ruby belongs to *Mars* and *Aries* and, since it is translucent, it acts on the higher centres of conscious thought, which become powerful and aggressive. The ruby strengthens intuition and initiative in thinking. Generally speaking, the ruby imparts energy, courage, passion and victory to its wearer. It repels enemies and diseases, strengthens the heart, purifies contaminated air, prevents decay, allays pain and agitation, helps against fever, phthisis and miscarriage and combats sloth and melancholia. It safeguards against floods, tempests and lightning. Catharine of Aragon had one that forewarned her of disaster.

The red colour makes one think of blood and there are in fact stories in which the ruby is associated with vampires. The so-called egg ruby of Parma played a tragic rôle in the evil deeds of the Borgias, but was apparently a spinel.

The ruby must be worn on the left-hand side. Water in which a ruby has lain for a long time, used to be employed as a means of healing and of restoring youth.

Some authorities assign the ruby to Capricorn and, if they are correct, it should win the favour of those in high office.

Sapphire

The sapphire can be white, light blue, blue-green or dark blue. The white or yellow kinds belong to Mercury and to its Signs, Gemini and Virgo. They give innocence and joy, calm nerves, thought concentration and helpful friends. They cure eye troubles, asthma, insomnia, effusions of blood and nervous disorders. Blue is the most characteristic colour. It belongs to *Venus* and her Sign, *Taurus*, which makes it the stone of *true friendship* or *love*. It gives devotion, fellow-feeling, chastity, veracity, imagination, faith, noble conduct, prophetic gift, peace of mind; it attracts good people and brings help in time of need, e.g. in fires and when one has lost one's way. It should be worn continuously on the chest underneath the clothing. For nose bleeds it is placed on the forehead. It makes the thoughts pure and genial, and is very suitable for use in meditation. It protects the eyes and heart, is a defence against black magic, and overcomes melancholy, fever and the effects of poisons.

The sapphire is the stone of yogis, healers, princes of the Church and saints. What is called sapphire in the Bible is lapis lazuli, however.

Just as in the ruby, colour changes in this stone are a warning that one is about to come into contact with calamities, treachery and poison. It protects against false friends.

The sapphire belongs to the disciple Thomas (when it is yellow) and to Jacob's son Dan.

There is a remarkable story concerning the talisman belonging to the wife of the Emperor Charlemagne, which was made for her by a magician from the retinue of Harun-al-Rashid. The talisman is said to have consisted of two uncut sapphires and a piece of the True Cross, the latter component being a somewhat unlikely sounding item for a Moslem to use. Charlemagne had given her the sapphires to secure their devotion to one another. When she died, Charlemagne could not bring himself to bury her, even when the body began to decay. It was only after his father confessor had removed the sapphires that he gave permission for the interment, but from that moment on his affection was transferred to his confessor whom he advanced to become archbishop of Mainz and Chancellor of the Empire. Not until he lay dying did the Emperor take back the stone from the priest and it was only then that he was able to die in peace.

Padparadschah
This is a reddish-yellow corundum, also named the *king topaz*, which comes from Sri Lanka. It belongs to Taurus. It makes people faithful, honest, cheerful and friendly, protects the wearer when travelling, gives knowledge of human nature and the ability to detect other people's evil intentions and therefore to see through false friends, and to sense when murder or poisoning is being attempted. It bestows honour, wealth and friendship, and is good for intestinal colic, a thick head, insomnia, restlessness and insanity.

Spinel
The spinel consists of crystallized pipe-clay and magnesium oxide (thus there is *no* aluminium in it) and its mother-stone is marble or dolomite, in which it is held in suspension. It belongs to the cubic system and forms octahedral crystals—two four-sided pyramids set base to base. It is always encountered when ore is washed with rubies and sapphires. Formerly, the distinction between this and the other stones was not so clearly understood and it was named the *balas ruby*. In nature, the spinel occurs in the colours red, blue, purple and brown. The yellow, green or colourless specimens are synthetic. There is a purple spinel with a trace of orange, which changes colour according to the lighting: in daylight it is blue but in artificial light it is violet.

The spinel or balas ruby we read about in old books going back to Roman times was a bright pink. The ruby-spinel was carmine red and the rubicelle a glowing orange-red. In India these three varieties were assigned to the three lower castes in the hierarchy of gems.

Since the fourteenth century, Europeans have learnt to distinguish the spinel ruby. A balas ruby was sometimes pawned by a prince and then later reclassified as a spinel, and thus a magnificent stone of some 300 carats say was suddenly and appallingly devalued. When Charles

IX of France pawned five large rubies from the royal treasury in 1569, among them the Côte de Bretagne, the valuers for the Duke of Florence stated that they were only balas rubies, and a balas ruby of 300 carats is worth less than a four carat pigeon blood ruby. The 415 carat ruby on top of the crown of the Czars of Russia is really a spinel. It is now on display in the Kremlin.

The Côte de Bretagne, a rose-pink balas ruby or spinel, was part of the dowry of Anne of Brittany when she wed Charles VIII of France in 1491; she wore it as a pendant. After she had been widowed, she later married another king of France, Louis XII. In 1749, Louis XVI had it cut into the form of a dragon. It disappeared with a great deal of other plunder during the Revolution, but came to light again and is now in the Louvre.

The celebrated balas ruby of 170 carats belonging to the English Black Prince was also a spinel. In 1397 the Prince acquired this stone from Dom Pedro of Castile. Henry V wore it on his helmet at the battle of Agincourt.

The dark red spinel makes a person strong and tough, as befits a stone of Mars and Saturn, but should definitely not be worn when Saturn is badly aspected.

The blue spinel calms sexual desire, brings good intentions to a successful issue and makes its wearer fearless and gives him faith and riches. It attracts help and assistance and is clearly influenced by Jupiter.

Zircon (Jacinth)

The zircon is a semi-precious stone crystallizing in the tetragonal system and coloured yellow to brown in nature. It is very plentiful in Sri Lanka and Indo-China and, in Bangkok, is made to change colour by undergoing heating to 850 to 1000 degrees Centigrade in the presence of air. It then turns blue and is made into jewellery.

It can also be made colourless and like diamond in appearance, and is marketed as the so-called *Matura diamond*. One difference from the real diamond is that whereas the diamond is singly refractive the zircon is doubly refractive, i.e. a single light ray passing through a zircon produces two rays and two spectra which are only partly overlapping. The zircon is also much softer than the diamond. Blue zircons are brittle and faded.

According to the tint, some zircons are known as *jacinths, jargons* and *starlites*. The fiery jacinth was greatly prized in antiquity and in the Middle Ages and was entered separately in lists of crown jewels. It was an orange-red stone, apparently its natural colour. Rudolf Steiner said that jacinth was the stone that developed in man the capacity to look into the spiritual world where he may see truths in the form of images and symbols. It works by means of the liver, the seat of our dream-thinking, our thinking in pictures; hence the jacinth is related to Sagittarius and Jupiter. Those who have projections of the astral body at night and are taken on a tour around the astral plane by a spirit guide, are instructed in pictures, but often contract some liver disorder as a consequence. On the other hand, doctors tell us that liver troubles are sometimes accompanied by hallucinations. In each case, the liver is the organ of picture-thinking, a mode of thinking which the jacinth is able to stimulate.

The old name jacinth, or hyacinth, has tended to be neglected recently. The varieties of zircon are known by their colour; jacinth being called the *orange zircon*.

Topaz

Topaz is not a quartz; it is an aluminium fluorine silicate found in granite and other igneous rocks. It has an irregular rhombic crystal form and occurs in the colours yellow, gold, red, blue and white. The yellow specimens contain chromium, the blue contain iron and the red vanadium.

The gold topazes have a certain amount of phosphorus as an impurity; they phosphoresce in the dark and wax and wane in power with the Moon, by which fact we immediately recognize that it is a stone of Sagittarius. This Moon-force in the stone promotes the growth of plant seed during the first quarter of the Moon. When set in the left horn of a breeding bull, it is said to increase its procreative power.

A genuine topaz worn in a golden necklace will ward off false friends, witchcraft and the evil eye, will benefit the activity of the liver and avert insomnia, nervousness and insanity. What is more, topazes have a good effect on the circulation of the blood, and prevent and cure haemorrhages, thromboses, varicose veins and haemorrhoids (piles). In other words they are good for relaxed and enfeebled veins. They promote blood heat and strengthen those parts that are cold and weak.

This stone gives chastity and happiness, keeps friends faithful and allays anger. On the approach of a thunderstorm it becomes strongly electric, making the wearer restless and sometimes, due to the raising of his potential, clairvoyant too. It restores the sense of taste to those who have lost it (co-operation here between the tongue and the liver) and can bestow eloquence. Many years ago, the topaz was frequently confused with other stones. The great 1680 carat stone named *Braganza*, which belongs to the Portuguese crown jewels, was once thought to be a diamond but is more likely to be a topaz.

The German imperial crown (woodcut of 1483).

Oriental topaz is another name for the yellow sapphire and Scottish topaz is *yellow quartz*. In Sri Lanka the colourless topaz is sold under the name of *water sapphire*. Topazes found in river gravel are so translucent that the French call them *gouttes d'eau* (water-drops).

The finest topazes come from Minas Geraes in Brazil.

19.

RED STONES

Garnet	Spessartite
Hessonite	Pyrope
Almandine	Haematite
Demantoid	Magnetite
Uvarovite	Rhodonite

Garnet

The magnificent red garnets are real stones of Mars. Their red coloration is mainly due to iron but sometimes due to manganese. They impart, power, energy, courage and intrepidity, also passionate love which may however turn to hatred. Wearing a garnet can lead to the break-up of a love affair. It gives a fondness for work plus perseverance but also pugnacity. In Italy it is worn by widows 'for consolation', meaning, in plain terms, that it helps them to capture a new mate.

Friends who have to part give one another garnets as keepsakes. This stone makes people clairvoyant, reveals hidden places and assists the discovery of buried treasure. It is a true Scorpio stone.

It fights the evil that lurks in the depths of the soul, and protects against impure thoughts, depression, diseases of the mind and heart, infection, inflammations and skin diseases. It is also a safeguard against being struck by lightning.

Garnet develops plastic imagery in man and gives a strong will, self-confidence, pride and success.

In the nineteenth century garnets were very much in fashion and they are commonly seen in brooches and bracelets that have been handed down as family heirlooms. They have always been a favourite form of jewellery; the ancient Egyptians used to wear them in necklaces and the ancient Greeks on their hands, shoulders and foreheads. In the Middle Ages they helped to fill the treasure chests of kings.

The word garnet is thought by some to have been given to the stone because its red colour resembles that of the pomegranate, while others think that both garnet and granite are derived from the Latin *granum*, a grain, garnet being chiefly found in the form of small round crystals in the matrix.

In addition to the red garnets (mainly pyrope and almandine) of which most jewellery is made, there are others with different colours such as green, yellow, orange, pink, reddish brown, reddish purple and black. Among these are *hessonite, almandine, demantoid, uvarovite, spessartite, pyrope* and *haematite*.

Hessonite (Cinnamon Stone)
Cinnamon stone is really a yellow to yellowish red variety of grossularite. It is sometimes a glowing orange colour and then makes beautiful jewellery.

Almandine
The Almandine is a purple-red stone belonging to Mars-Jupiter. It mainly occurs in Sri Lanka, but also in India, Australia, Madagascar, Uruguay and in many states of North America. It contains iron and aluminium, but sometimes the iron is replaced by magnesium or manganese, and then the stone is more like pyrope and spessartite and is by way of being an intermediate form. The almandine is a semi-precious stone, red at times like a 'bottle of Bordeaux wine in the shade' but at its best when strongly illuminated.

Some have thought that the famous light-giving mediaeval 'carbuncle' was an almandine.

Demantoid
This is a glorious green stone with a fire so strong that it ranks next to that of diamond and sphene. The green, which is due to chromium oxide is fine and transparent. It is usually found in small pieces of two or three carats on the west side of the Urals south of Sverdlovsk

(formerly Yekaterinburg) in the stream Bobrovska.

Demantoids are at their best when cut as brilliants.

Uvarovite

This is another green garnet from the Urals with splendid fiery crystals that are unfortunately too small to cut. It is a combination of calcium and chromium occurring in some serpentines and in limestones associated with chromium ores. Another area in which it is found is California.

Spessartite

This garnet contains manganese and aluminium. The manganese imparts to its twelve-sided crystals a beautiful violet hue which makes it desirable as a semi-precious stone.

Pyrope

Pyrope is a bright red garnet, much employed in ecclesiastical jewellery, in which it gives the impression of costly rubies since the colours of the two types of stone is much the same. It occurs in the so-called blue pipes of Kimberley and is marketed as *Cape ruby*, just as pyrope from Arizona is sold under the name of *Arizona ruby*.

It is a magnesium-aluminium garnet and is usually given a convex shape with a hollow lower surface, in order to make it translucent. The main centres where it is worked are the small towns of Turnau and Gablonz in Bohemia. Some people think that pyrope is the carbuncle to which reference is made in old stories, e.g. in the account in the Talmud claiming that Noah's ark was illuminated by one enormous garnet. Pyrope and almandine strengthen the heart and intellect and attract inspiration.

Haematite

Haematite, the Dutch bloodstone, is not the same as the English bloodstone or heliotrope.

Haematite appears as nodules embedded in red ironstone. They start as a gel and resemble animal organs such as the kidneys, lungs or liver. A dark red-grey in colour, haematite has a gloss as if it were lacquered. The stone is fibrous in character and therefore hard to polish. When it is being worked, the cherry-red powder turns the jet of water played on it as red as blood; hence the name given to it in The Netherlands (blood stone).

The doctrine of signatures suggests that on this account haematite ought to make a good styptic, and so it is not surprising that soldiers like to carry a piece with them into battle. It strengthens the heart, imparts courage and endurance, protects from danger and blesses with peaceful sleep. It is good for a rapid pulse, bloodshot eyes, ulcers, and cramp in the calf muscles. The powder helps in kidney and bladder diseases.

Haematite is also found in crystals but it is only the nodules which are worked into ringstones, cuff-links, pendants etc. The darker haematite is made into beads and these are sometimes passed off as black pearls.

Engraved pieces of haematite are found in ancient Egyptian tombs and in the mines of Babylon. In Mexico and South America, Spain and France, haematite is cut in intaglio and set in jewellery.

Magnetite

Magnetite is a black ore that is found both in dark octahedral crystals and in amorphous lumps, and can be attracted by a magnet from the surrounding rubble. On account of this power it has also been called *Hercules stone*. It is said to draw shrapnel from wounds.

In 2634 B.C., the Chinese emperor Huang-ti constructed a compass with the aid of this stone, while in twelfth-century Europe the Vikings were making magnetic needles.

Throughout antiquity it was recognized that this stone had the power to cure rheumatism, weakness, liver and eye diseases, fractures, leg cramp, and barrenness in women. Neuralgia can be cured by stroking the temples with it.

Magnetite is said to bestow on orators eloquence and convincing power.

It promotes harmony between brothers and in marriage and is therefore set in wedding rings. In a Roman temple there once stood a magnetite statue of Venus and an iron statue of Mars which were said to move towards one another during marriage ceremonies. In India, magnetite is worn as the stone that imparts strength and health and the Mahometans employ it to drive away evil spirits, in other words as an amulet.

Mars and Saturn work together in magnetite just as in red spinel (mentioned elsewhere) which has the same crystalline form: an octahedron. Although not red, magnetite fits into the same group.

Rhodonite

Rhodonite (manganese silicate) is pink with black veins of brown-stone. It occurs in large flat crystals (triclinic system). The sources of this stone are the Urals and Sweden and, for flesh-coloured sorts, Massachusetts in the USA and Australia. When a fine polish has been imparted to it, the opaque sort is employed to cover mantlepieces and the like. Those that are translucent or, in some cases, practically transparent, are cut into cabochons. Unfortunately they grow darker on exposure to light.

The pink *rhodochrosite* (manganese spar) can also have a delightful tint.

Manganese, which is related to iron, is good for mental unrest and confusion, anxious forebodings and incoherence. In other words, it fends off influences from the etheric plane. It is the stone for mediumistic people who would prefer to be left in peace.

20.

THE HOLY BLUE AND GREEN STONES

Chrysolite (peridot, olivine)   Vesuvianite
Serpentine   Malachite
Jade   Azurite
Nephrite   Turquoise
Diopside   Tourmaline
Epidote   Lapis lazuli

Many ancient races, such as the Chinese, considered green stones to be holy and had a deep veneration for them. In part, these are the stones that developed in the period when the vegetable life forces (Moon) exerted their greatest influence on earth. The rocks were still soft, the atmosphere was humid and the Moon had not yet left the earth. Plants which now are no more than one and a half feet high, then towered up to heights of thirty or sixty feet or more, and the surface of the earth was covered by a lush carpet of leaves in the form of tree-ferns, horse-tails and similar plants. In those strata we know as slate and gneiss the minerals adopted more or less vegetable-like, foliated forms. We are referring to minerals such as serpentine asbestos, chrysotile, gabbro, diorite and diabase. *Magnesium* plays a big part in these rocks, the very magnesium that is an essential component of chlorophyll in plants with green leaves, which use it to harness the power of sunlight. These minerals consist mainly of magnesium silicate and their green colour is due to bivalent iron. Often they resemble wood or leaves, and some varieties have actually been called mountain wood and mountain cork. At a later stage, when the Moon had left the Earth and the life-forms on Earth had started to dry up and shrink in size (owing to the polar action of the Moon and Saturn), minerals began to become more ligneous, horny and rocky.

Chrysolite (olivine, peridot), spinel (not always green), serpentine and nephrite are rich in magnesium.

The holy stone of the Aztecs in old Mexico was the emerald, and the sacred stones of Ancient China were *aventurine* (in which the imperial seal was cut), *green jade* and *nephrite*, all of them classed as sacred Yu stones.

In ancient Egypt, considerable importance was attached to the copper ore malachite (other stones which contain copper are chrysocolla, azurite and dioptase).

Examples of greenish blue stones are *turquoise*, and *amazonite*, while *labradorite*, *azurite* and *lapis lazuli* are almost pure blue.

The *aquamarine* is a greenish blue, the *tourmaline* is pink on top and greenish blue underneath, and the *chrysoprase* is pure light green.

Chrysolite (Olivine, Peridot)

The magnesium-rich chrysolite is a stone of the *Sun*, and therefore of the *eye*. It is not surprising that it improves the eyesight. On occasions its green 'eyes' stare at us from basalt breakwaters.

Chrysolite is a silicate of magnesium with iron and some nickel and manganese. Being fairly soft, it is unsuitable for rings. It is the only gem to be found in meteorites, for instance in the enormous meteor found at Krasnoyarsk in 1749. Because the minerals and metals present in green stones also occur in meteorites, green stones came to be regarded as *heavenly*.

When the Sun, Earth and Moon were still one, these stones received a *potential existence* through the Sun-force which also works in the diamond and in gold. This is the power of *light*, and we can consider these stones together with magnesium and gold as gifts from the Sun sent to us Earth creatures to remind us of our royal lineage. In other words, these things help us to open our inner sight to the spiritual Sun. Sun-spots are the places where the Sun is ejecting luminous matter which will one day become meteorites. The latter are the petrified radiance that invests all solar entities that have left the Sun. The individual who has a feeling for precious stones can sense a little of the forces that lie imprisoned in their dense forms. The cosmic materials reaching the Earth in the form of meteorites are invariably given by our Sun and come in the guise of iron, magnesium and silica. It is the silica and magnesium in plants that make them responsive to sunlight. Iron and silica make the living human skin sensitive to the solar rays.

Chrysolite—which is more often known as *olivine* on account of its olive-green colour—is thus a very ancient stone and is very plentiful in its natural state; however the orthorhombic crystals that are big enough to cut are hard to come by. The stone comes in two colours: the golden (*chrysos* = gold) and the true green. The latter is so full of light that it seems to radiate even when placed in the shadow. It shows to equal advantage in artificial light and in daylight.

Around 1500 B.C. the golden variety was discovered in the volcanic peridot on the Red Sea island of Zeberged (the Island of St John) and became known as the *stone of the Sun*. The gem was so highly valued that the government made the island a restricted area and compelled the inhabitants to toil in the mines, where they frequently died of hunger and snakebite. The reptiles seemed to guard this treasure and from time to time the Pharaoh ordered a grand clearance of serpents.

Golden olivine or peridot is apparently the 'topaz' of the historian Pliny. Green olivine, on the other hand, was not known in Europe until long after Pliny's time; it seems that the Crusaders returned with it from the Near East and presented specimens to Church and State under the misapprehension that they were emeralds.

Olivines worth cutting are found not only on Zeberged but also in Bohemia, the Eifel region of the Rhine, in British Columbia and in Arizona.

A homoeopathic attenuation of crude chrysolite is prescribed for eye complaints. In addition to benefiting external sight, this stone also helps inner vision and the ability to look into the future. It relieves the wearer of melancholia and delusions and gives him inspiration and eloquence.

Serpentine

Some metamorphic rocks consist almost entirely of great beds of this secondary mineral. Its fibrous form is asbestos. Serpentine occurs in creamy white, many shades of green and in black. It has a waxy shine and feels greasy, just like soap-stone. Sometimes it is fluorescent.

The Lizard area in Cornwall is a source of serpentine and there it is made into pretty little vases and trays. Big ornaments can also be cut from it with the steel saw and serpentine is even used for building-stone in some districts. Cameos are made from it too. The rough stone often contains white veins of steatite, and dark-green pieces with black flecks and worn smooth and round by the sea are to be found on pebbly beaches.

Varieties of serpentine are:

Verdite, green with brown and yellow-green stripes. Bead necklaces are made from it. It is mined in the Barberton district of The Transvaal.

Bowenite, apple-green to yellow-white. Found in India, New Zealand, Afghanistan and the USA. Knife handles are made from it.

Williamsite, greenish, found in the USA.

Antigorite, dark green, mined in Italy.

Connemara marble, green with white flecks or veins of calcite. This is very common in Ireland and is made into beads and all sorts of jewellery.

Jade

Jade rivals nephrite as one of the strongest of stones, which can withstand a greater pressure than steel. In olden days, spear points, axe heads and knives were made from it. The builders of the Swiss lake-dwellings had a liking for it as long ago as 1500 B.C., and the Egyptians were using it around the same time. In Ancient Mexico, the Mayas used to cut whole scenes out of jade, sacerdotal images which have been excavated at the sites of ruined temples, also thousands of jade beads and tablets. Jadeite does not contain magnesium but is a sodium and aluminium silicate, mixed with silicates of iron and chromium which impart the green colour to it: the emerald green is due to chromium and the bottle green to iron. Violet shades also occur due to the presence of manganese. The best jades come from the Katchin mountains in Upper Burma, where they are found in association with enormous layers of serpentine. Also jadeite is found in Eastern Turkestan and in the region of the Pamirs. The jade used to make Egyptian scarabs once came from the Greek island of Syra. Jade has also been found in Canada and the USA, in New Zealand and in Silesia.

The name jade derives from the Spanish expression, *piedra de ijada* or colic stone. What happened was that the conquistadors saw the Mexicans using both jade and nephrite as a remedy for the kidneys. In China, jade was honoured as the best of all precious stones and as a symbol of the five chief virtues: mercy, modesty, courage, justice and wisdom. The so-called Imperial Jade is emerald green, shining and perfect. It gets its name from the fact that it was the favourite stone of the last Empress of China (who had to give way to the republicans in 1912). Each piece that was found had to be submitted to her and even the specimens she rejected qualified as imperial. She collected 3000 ivory cabinets full of this green jade. One piece went with her at all times so that she could play with it in her fingers and so quiet her inner restlessness. (In much the same way, the Arabs and Greeks toy with their carnelian worry beads.) Besides being queen, jade also occurs in soft lavender blue, grey and bright orange.

Jade is not sold in the same way as are other precious stones in rough crystals. A piece of jadeite is a block of rock and the purchaser has no means of telling by eye how thick the green layer is. Such a lump was sold for 100,000 dollars recently; which must have involved a high risk factor. In former times, a block like this was split up by heating it strongly and then plunging it in cold water so that it burst open. Nowadays the job is done with a diamond saw.

A great many useful properties have been ascribed to jade. It is said to prolong life, help childbirth, protect from accidents, give a large family and engender luck in games of chance. It is clearly a stone of Venus and the Moon and belongs to the Fifth House of the horoscope.

Nephrite

Nephrite is closely related to jade. It has a silky sheen owing to the fine fibres in its structure and is a lovely soft green in colour. This stone does not consist of single crystals but of an aggregate of small crystals, among them actinolite. It is a calcium and magnesium silicate with iron silicate and pipe-clay. The microscopically small crystals intermingle in a tough coherent mass, so that nephrite was successfully used in ancient times as a material for tools, weapons and talismans. Nephrite axes are found in palaeolithic sites all over the world. They used to be tied to their wooden helves with strips of leather. Large blocks of nephrite are too hard to work with hammer and chisel. In China they are heated and then thrown into cold water; they can then be split along the resulting cracks.

In New Zealand the Maoris cut their talisman, the Tiki, out of jade or nephrite. This was a manikin with its head turned to one side in a listening attitude. It was worn suspended from the neck and was thought to contain all the qualities and luck of the tribe, being handed down from father to son until it was eventually buried with the last of the line. The Maoris also made weapons, tools and jewellery from nephrite. Tamerlane's mortuary monument in Samarkand consists of a block of nephrite. In Eastern Turkestan it is found in the high mountains of the Kwen Lun.*

This stone is beneficial to the kidneys. A little book was brought out in Delft in 1674 by Outger Cluijt on the 'Properties, Powers and Effects of the Lapis nephriticus, etc.'. He relates that the physician Paludanus of Enkhuizen in the Netherlands possessed an American nephrite which was so beneficial in renal colic and stone that in two of his patients who did no more than wear the stone on their bodies, so many stones and so much sediment was passed that they had to take it off for a while every now and again. The Spanish physician Monardes informs us of a nobleman who wore a nephrite bracelet and discharged a mass of kidney stones. As soon as he took the bangle off the discharge stopped and as soon as he put it on again the cleansing activity recommenced. By wearing a nephrite the Countess of Bejar was free for ten years from the renal colic from which she had regularly suffered before.

Diopside

This is a stone that forms magnificent bottle-green crystals. It occurs in the Alatal and Zillertal for instance, where it is found together with garnets, also in North and South America and in the Blue Ground in South Africa, which is diamond country. The dark green chromium-rich diopside is cut and polished.

Epidote

This green stone is found in the Pinzgau in Salzburg. It is a silicate of calcium, aluminium and iron that grows in mountain wool, a felty form of asbestos with a give like leather when pressed by the fingers.

Manganese epidote found in Piedmont is red in colour due to its manganese content.

---

*The Kwen Lun mountains are in Tibet. *Translator's note.*

Vesuvianite or Idocrase

This stone was originally found in the lava of Vesuvius. It forms green and brown crystals and also jade-like masses. It comes in all sorts of colour variations.

Malachite

Malachite is a noble copper ore, consisting of copper carbonate plus 8 per cent water. The verdigris on the copper cupolas found on certain church buildings is formed when the copper combines chemically with the carbonic acid in the air, and this green patina which prevents further corrosion by the air also occurs in malachite, although it often looks black in its natural state. Like agate, it is built up of different layers and it exhibits asterism due to the fine fibres running through it. By special cutting, the stone can be made to exhibit light concentric circles around a darker centre—the so-called *eye malachite*.

In Ancient Egypt the malachite was greatly in demand. The ladies used it for making up their eyes, lashes, eyebrows and hair. Imhotep, the celebrated physician and vizier, discovered that this substance was beneficial to the eyes as well. He had malachite mixed with the excrement of a cat or cow or of flies and laid this as a compress on diseased eyes, where it had to be left for four days. This apparently cured the terrible Egyptian eye troubles!

The copper in malachite also has a curative action on cholera, colic, asthma, cardiac spasm, irregular menstruation, wounds, toothache and poisoning. Malachite promotes lactation, makes longings less poignant and gives hope. It is a stone of Venus and, in a special sense, of the Moon in Taurus. Cut in the shape of a heart, it is worn for comfort by those who are unlucky in love. It strengthens the heart. Anyone drinking from a malachite beaker is said to be able to understand the language of the animals.

Enormous blocks of malachite have been found in the Urals at Yekaterinburg and at Nizhniy Tagil, where one weighed nearly 25 tons. Dishes, vases and chandeliers, table tops, mantle-pieces and magnificent casings for pillars were made of malachite when the Czars ruled Russia. The columns in St Isaac's Cathedral, Leningrad (old St Petersburg), are covered with malachite. The same feature was introduced into the Ayasofya (St Sophia) in Istanbul and into the Temple of Diana at Ephesus. Much of our present-day malachite is imported from Katanga, Australia and Chile.

Azurite

Azurite is a copper carbonate which occurs in gleaming blue crystals and contains only 5 per cent water. However, if it absorbs water it will change into malachite. Through such a pseudo-morphosis a certain amount of carbon dioxide disappears and the originally transparent azurite crystals become green and opaque.

This azurite-cum-malachite occurs in stalactite form in the Arizona copper mines, and when cut as a cabochon the mixed stone takes on the appearance of a peacock's feather. It is very appropriate to Aquarius.

Turquoise

The sky-blue or green-blue turquoise is a soft stone which, like malachite and haematite, is a gel that has been converted to a crystalline structure. The gel condition is that of living matter and represents that period in the Earth's history when minerals were plastic and much more 'living', much more plant-like. Hence there is more 'life' in turquoise than in the harder minerals. In the said period, the Earth and Sun were still united and so there is still a degree of solar energy stored in the turquoise, even though it does not contain magnesium. It is a complex of copper and aluminium phosphates with the addition of some silica, ammonia and water. It is granular, fibrous and opaque and consists of microscopically small crystals. In layers of grape- or kidney-shaped stones it covers weathered rock in volcanic areas. It occurs in Mexico, Iran, Tibet and Afghanistan and at Samarkand; also in Egypt and in the Sinai Peninsula, where the Egyptians were gathering turquoise as long ago as 4000 B.C. The Egyptians felt an affinity for turquoise, lapis lazuli and malachite, as stones in which the very earthy clay joined the more heavenly, sunny, colourful and light-giving copper and phosphorus. In other words, they saw them as stones where Heaven met Earth.

The sky-blue varieties belong to the Sun and Venus (copper), the ice-blue to Saturn and the green-blue to Uranus and its sign Aquarius. Turquoise is a sensitive stone which has to be protected from sunlight, heat, perspiration, grease, perfume, dirt, soap and caustic liquids. It loses colour when its wearer is ill or in danger; for example, a green-blue turquoise worn by a patient with liver trouble will turn a dull yellow.

If the wearer is menaced by misfortune, this stone attracts the evil to itself and absorbs the harmful vibrations, sometimes being shattered under the strain. Because turquoise is reputed to avert the evil eye, a string of turquoise beads is often hung round the neck of a child.

The turquoise was the sacred stone of the Persians during the time of Zoroaster (purity).* It reached Europe from Iran *via* Turkey; hence its name, for turquoise stands for 'Turkish stone'. In the Orient it is thought to protect riders and their steeds (Jupiter, Sagittarius); strings of turquoise beads are attached to horses' harness in order to make them sure-footed on the narrow mountain paths. Boeotius de Boot tells how he used to own a turquoise which lost its colour, however, shortly before his horse slipped and fell ten feet without suffering any injury; the stone itself split in two.

The sky-blue variety has a similar action to that of the sapphire and is a stone for young girls and true love and innocence. It defends the virtuous. In Russia the peasant will give a turquoise set in a silver ring to his bride. It gives the woman peace of mind and is said to give the man strength for labour, prosperity, popularity and health.

The Arabs wear a turquoise between three pearls on their turbans. When it is the hour of Jupiter they take the stone in their right hands and make their wishes on it while gazing at it fixedly. It is also suitable for meditation. It must be given, not bought.

Tourmaline

Tourmaline is a notable stone, which occurs in different colours on its way from darkness to light.

An examination of granite, the commonest rock in the earth's crust, shows that it is composed of quartz, feldspar, mica and hornblende. The quartz contains that *light*-element from which, as we have seen, many transparent and translucent precious stones have been formed. Feldspar is the element of *colour*, which arose from the same cosmic powers as the sex organs in flowers did; to feldspar belong the *moonstone, sunstone, amazonite* and *labradorite*. Mica imparts *glitter*. Hornblende, however, occurs in fine, pitch-black needles, completely opaque and dull.

Chemical changes in the dark hornblende produce tourmaline. Borium enters the needles and the latter rise through the granite or flint in bundles, illustrating the upward-striving force that works in tourmaline. It starts in the dark depths of the Earth's crust where the

---

*The name Zoroaster or Zarathustra has a more esoteric meaning than this.
                                                                Translator's note.

form of matter—the cross-form (life ether, Saturn)—appears. For example, we find there the four-sided prisms of *andalusite*, which stick out of flint rock at top and sides. Andalusite is an aluminium silicate. Another stone in the dark depths is the so-called *Cross-stone, harmotome* or *chiastolite*, which when cut exhibits a black St Andrew's Cross. *Staurolite* is different again. An iron and aluminium silicate, it appears in twin crystals which sometimes make an acute angle to one another but sometimes stand at right angles and form a cross of anything up to 1.2 inches long. Such crosses are sold as talismans and souvenirs.

But tourmaline is not simply ruled by the life ether; it has the typical roundedness of the warmth ether too, and occurs in three- to nine-sided ribbed columns reminiscent of plant stalks. Here again, there is an affinity with the vegetable world. The old Sun is still active in it, therefore, but it also glows with the many colours bestowed on flowers by the Sun in the sky. Tourmaline is often green underneath and pink on top. The tingeing metals diffuse slowly towards the interior of the growing stone but sometimes fail to reach its centre, which is left clear. A crystal of this sort can contain as many as twenty different constituents, including calcium, magnesium, silica, clay, boron and fluorides. When iron is present the tourmalines are green or blue; chromium gives an emerald green shade and cobalt a violet one as in the so-called *rubellite*.

Pink tourmaline is known as *apyrite*, the brown as *dravite* and the blue as *indigolite*.

Green, yellow-green and honey-yellow stones come from Sri Lanka. The Zillertal in the Tyrol is a source of black tourmaline or *schorl*, crystals of which can attain a length of as much as 80 feet. This is used for mourning jewellery. Sometimes the form follows lines of radiation to produce so-called tourmaline suns.

At the beginning of the eighteenth century, Dutch venturers brought the tourmaline back from Sri Lanka, where it was called turmali. They found it useful for cleaning their old-fashioned clay pipes: if the tourmaline was rubbed with a scrap of woollen material or was merely warmed, it became charged with static electricity (being positive at the end with many small facets and negative at the other end) and could then be used for drawing out the tobacco ash. Apart from Sri Lanka, tourmaline is mainly found in America, Africa, Madagascar and the Urals.

It is clear then that tourmaline carries many powers within it: the petrifying power of the cross, the light force of the ternary, the warmth of roundedness, electric power and the upward-striving power. Some people claim that the latter power can be employed to help toddlers who fall over a lot when trying to walk by hanging a piece of the stone in a woollen bag around their necks. What is more *all* the colours are present in tourmaline. Not only can the various colours be seen in a single stone from top to bottom but also from inside to outside. Green and red are occasionally seen alternating in triangles. Some stones are green inside and red outside or *vice versa*.

People in the Middle Ages were fond of using tourmalines that were black at the bottom and red at the top as meditation stones; Rosicrucians and alchemists called them *Christus-stones*, and regarded them as symbolizing the ascent from matter through the multicoloured phenomena of the soul to the rose red of sublime love.

Tourmaline is a solar stone which attracts inspiration, goodwill and friendship and bestows self-confidence and joy of life. It, so to speak, overcomes Saturn by means of the Sun. The luminous *carbuncle* which figures so mysteriously in mediaeval manuscripts is usually a red gem of some sort, more often than not a red tourmaline. In those days it was cut as a cabochon and had a rounded surface. The old Jews called it bareqeth or 'lightning stone'. It was said to shine in the dark and Noah was supposed to have taken a large one into the ark. Reputedly, it can arrest the decomposition of dead bodies, cure infectious diseases, blood poisoning, consumption and plague, suppress sensuality and dispel grief and evil thoughts. It reconciles friends, wards off enemies, calms the nervous and gives inspiration, concentration and eloquence. Sometimes it is associated with Mercury and Gemini.

Lapis Lazuli

The sky-blue lapis lazuli is another of the sacred stones. The Ancient Egyptians called it the Stone of the Heavens. It occurs in lands with the oldest cultures, such as Egypt and Mexico. For instance, it is to be found in the Cordilleras of the Andes 11,500 feet above sea level in mountains which were once flatlands washed by the sea. The most productive sources are the shores of Lake Baikal, North West Afghanistan and Burma.

The blue colour is a sort of celestial sulphur which still floated in the atmosphere in Lemurian times and subsequently solidified into this stone. It is granular in structure, forms occasional crystals and occurs in limestone in the middle of granite. Its components are *sodalite* (a sodium and aluminium silicate with sodium chloride), *haüyne* (a sodium and aluminium silicate with calcium sulphate) and *lazurite* (sodium and aluminium silicate with sodium sulphide). Specks of pyrites show that what we have is genuine lapis lazuli.

While on his travels in 1271, Marco Polo came across mines of lapis lazuli in Siberia and Afghanistan which he thought might have been worked for 5000 years. They were worked in the winter and fires were lit near by for heating the stones so that cold water could be thrown over them to start to break them up. The miners then split them into smaller pieces with hammers and pick-axes. The stone is exported to Germany, Russia, China and India, where it is made into rings, brooches, beads and ear-drops, also vases and basins, knife-handles and inlaid work. Beautiful examples are to be found in the old churches and palaces of Russia. Catherine II covered the walls of a ballroom in her palace of Zarskoie-Selo with lapis lazuli and amber. Altars and pillars in old Italian and Spanish churches were decorated with this material too.

A very old practice was to employ powdered lapis lazuli as the pigment *ultramarine*. This expensive paint, used in old paintings, is now imitated with china clay, coal, sulphur and sodium carbonate. The Egyptians modelled scarabs in it.

Lapis lazuli was the favourite stone of Louis XIV of France, also of the unfortunate Bavarian king Ludwig II, who had table tops and cupboards made of it.

It is a stone of the Sun and Jupiter, it strengthens the power of radiation of the will, kindness and helpfulness. It protects from evil influences and is decidedly a *stone of friendship*. Also it promotes social work in general.

Lapis lazuli helps against depression. When warmed, it is applied to swellings and painful nerves. It can be left in warm water for a few minutes and then this water can be used as an eyewash (the doctrine of signatures has no bearing here and should not be taken as guidance on suitability for certain colours of eyes).

When set in a ring, it gives healthy blood, a cheerful frame of mind and deep, sound sleep which is not easily disturbed. Shy children can wear it round their necks to give them more self-confidence. It is recommended for the heart and spleen, blood and skin, and against epilepsy and strokes.

Lapis lazuli increases love and in some countries was devoted to Venus and later to the Virgin Mary, but it also has Uranian vibrations. In olden times, lapis lazuli was prized as a very costly stone, which was then known as sapphire. So it adorned the breastplate of the high priest of Israel and that of the Egyptian high priest at Memphis; it was sacred to the Assyrians and lined the walls of the palace of the king of Tyre. It was also much used for signet rings.

Crapaudina, the toadstone.

The troops of Alexander the Great brought it with them to Europe. A great deal of hidden activity goes on in Badakshan in Afghanistan now as in the past; there are no really passable roads to the mines, which are guarded by peaks, precipices, avalanches, bitter cold and snow, not to speak of the wary Afghan officials who have to be persuaded to issue visas.

21.

FELDSPARS

Moonstone
Sunstone
Amazonite
Labradorite

Feldspars make up the largest group of minerals and are found in all volcanic rocks. They are aluminium silicates with several other metals in combination. Usually they are smooth with a glassy or pearly lustre.

Granite consists of quartz, mica and feldspar. According to Rudolf Steiner, mica, as a survival from the period when minerals were still 'living' and plant-like, is related to the sepals of plants and, in the same manner, feldspar is related to their pistils or stigmas. What is more, the colours in granite are due to feldspar. These colours are those of metals such as iron, but are also attributable to the segregation of the various components of the feldspar, with one part for instance being deposited in fine platelets or crystals, and so on. The result is a sheen created in the same way as is the mother-of-pearl in the oyster shell. Some petals exhibit the same type of sheen.

A feldspar crystal can be cleaved in two mutually perpendicular planes. When the angle is exactly ninety degrees, we have orthoclase (= right-angled splitter). If the deviation from this is less than half a degree, we have microcline (= hardly sloping). In all other cases the size of the angle of cleavage is around eighty-six degrees, and then we speak of plagioclase (= oblique splitter).

When homogeneous crystals separate out on cooling, so that a part containing potassium is divided from another part containing sodium, the stone becomes dipolar as it were, and we have that perthite structure clearly seen in the moonstone.

Moonstone

This stone is mainly found in weathered rocks in Sri Lanka. Earlier, it was also obtained from the St Gotthard area in Switzerland. Other sources are in Burma, Australia and America. The bluish sheen of this stone arises through the process of segregation by which, in this case, the sodium feldspar separates from the potassium feldspar and is laid down in thin plates according to its own structure. The finer the lamellae, the more intense is the bluish light. Heating interferes with this arrangement and the lustre disappears.

Moonstone is a potassium and aluminium silicate and therefore, a silica compound. It is also called water opal, fish eye or wolf's eye.*

It changes with the phases of the moon. When the moon is waxing it is good for consumptives and when the moon is waning it helps one to look into the future. When a moonstone is held in the mouth, it is said that the things that should be done are more clearly impressed on the conscious mind, while those things that should not be done fade from the memory. If the stone is hung on the branches of a blossoming fruit-tree when the moon is increasing in light, it is believed that the crop of fruit will be plentiful. Arab women stitch it into their clothing so that they will be blessed with children. In India, whose land and people are ruled by Cancer the Sign of the Moon, it is the sacred stone, the dream-stone. It is thought there that the best specimens are washed up by the river when Sun and Moon are in good aspect, and the finest of all only once in twenty-one years. The moonstone favours sweethearts in the waxing moon. It gives inspiration and success in love, encourages personal attachments, unmasks enemies, ennobles the emotional life and protects from dropsy. All these things are very much to do with the Moon.

Sunstone

This is a translucent, reddish plagioclase in which, through a process of segregation, small flakes of haematite have formed. When the stone is

---

*Selenite is also mentioned, but this is a different type of stone.

Translator's note.

illuminated, these reflect red and yellow flashes of light. There are whitish, brownish and greenish sunstones, all of them speckled.

Sunstone is a sodium-calcium plagioclase and its crystals belong to the triclinic system. Usually, however, it is found in large blocks. At times twinned crystals are found.

The sunstone is sometimes confused with aventurine quartz, but the latter is harder, dark green, and has black inclusions. The so-called goldstone is synthetic; it is glass with copper particles as inclusions, and was formerly taken for sunstone. Genuine sunstone was originally found on an island in the White Sea at the end of the eighteenth century. Later on a sunstone with a gold lustre was found at Lake Baikal, and then in North America.

Amazonite

Amazonite stone is formed as unusually large crystals in the pergamite stage of granite. It is a potassium feldspar which is green due to its copper content. Now, copper occupies a place in the blood of crustaceans that is analogous to that occupied by iron in the blood of red-blooded animals. In the pegmatite layers, copper has a similar function to the one it has in the shells of simple marine animals. Copper occurs in those places where the remains of dead crustaceans have been deposited on the floor of the ocean. The same cosmic force that combines copper and lime in crustaceans, combines them in amazonite.

Amazonite is another of the sacred green stones, and was much employed and valued by the Ancient Egyptians. The most beautiful specimens come from the Urals. Others are found in South West Africa. Madagascar and America (Colorado).

Labradorite

This is an iridescent blue stone, a potassium and sodium feldspar, which is sometimes mixed with magnetite or titanic iron ore, giving points of light on the polished upper surface of the stone. The colours, blue and green, or yellow and red, glint brilliantly and move over the stone when it is turned round. Although the stone itself is opaque, the colours shimmer as marvellously as those in a butterfly's wing and it looks as if the stone is radiating light. This radiance has been preserved from the time when the Earth was still united with the Sun and, in a way, it is ancient sunlight from the Hyperborean period, if we may be permitted to borrow the name given to northern lands by the Ancient Greeks. Labradorite does in fact come from the north, from the coast of Labrador, from North America, from Finland and from the district around Leningrad. The stone is used to make ornaments. It belongs to Jupiter and Sagittarius and is worn as a talisman.

22.

DIAMONDS AND
RELATED STONES

Diamond
Jet
Pyrites
Marcasite

Diamonds
The cubic crystals of the diamond are made of pure crystallized *carbon*. This substance belongs to the vegetable kingdom, where it combines with water to form starch and sugar (carbohydrates), and to the action of the life ether and of the contracting and hardening power of Saturn. Hence it belongs to the melancholy temperament, to the strict moral law, to an awareness of sin and guilt, to increasing rigidity and to blackness.

It is well known that dead vegetable matter can turn, stage by stage, into *humus, peat, lignite, pit-coal, graphite* and *diamond*. The influence of Saturn on living plants eventually produces diamond, the hardest of all stones. This pathway lies, so to speak, between the Sun and Saturn, between life and death, between light and darkness.

The toughest form is the black diamond or *carbonado* or *bort*, which is black and opaque and often encountered in purely spherical lumps ranging in size from that of a pea to that of an egg and having a shiny surface. The shape is that of the Sun and the colour is that of Saturn. Life starts as a sphere. *Graphite* (from which 'lead' pencils are made) is carbon in the form of flaky layers rather like those of mica; it is evident that the same cosmic force is at work in it, namely that of the Moon, but in a different period, because graphite appears instead of mica in the same types of rock in the same circumstances (i.e. in granite, gneiss and slate) as the mica did formerly. Even a woody type of graphite is found in Sri Lanka, and the vessels in it radiate outwards like the beams of the Sun. This is a phenomenon of life and is seen in the annual rings of tree trunks.

As a matter of fact, diamonds are usually found in the company of the green stones, especially of chrysolite (olivine), in which the life forces of the Moon can still be clearly detected. In a manner of speaking, the diamond has shaken off the influence of the Moon. The formation of the diamond follows the same process as is carried on in man when he draws abstract truth from concrete experiences and discards the material by which he learned while preserving the pure abstraction. Thus man distances himself from his life-pole in order to worship God in *spirit* and in *truth*. Diamond, therefore, is appropriate to the Jewish-Calvanistic soul-structure, which is why it has become the most valued stone in our own era. In the Middle Ages the term used was *adamant* (from *adamas*) meaning untamable.

The applying conjunction of the Moon and Saturn is typical of these people: the life-pole is sacrificed to the thought-pole, and so the diamond is formed from and fed by the life-forces in the green sunstones and the so-called *blue ground*. It holds itself haughtily aloof from its origins in order to concentrate on perfecting its inner being. It might be said that the diamond is an expression of *pure spirit*.

So diamonds are sometimes round and sometimes roundish dodecahedra and octahedra (four-sided double pyramids): the roundedness of the Sun and the four-squareness of Saturn. Diamond shapes hover between the Sun and Saturn, between spirit and matter.

Since 1867, the most important source of diamonds has been South Africa, where the blue ground, or Kimberlite, occurs in volcanic pipes; this can be blasted to disengage the harder and thus undamaged diamonds. The rubble is washed in a stream of water over greased shakers, to which the diamonds adhere, whereas the other minerals are carried away. Diamonds were later discovered in *yellow ground*, which seems to be weathered blue ground. They are often sieved out of ore-wash. Tinted diamonds are blue, yellow or pink. In the first half-century of diamond mining in South Africa, twenty-four stones between 100 and 1600 carats were found (1 carat = 3.086 grains).

Prior to this, very fine diamonds were found in India and Brazil. A famous example was the *The Great Mogul*, a blue-green diamond of 400 carats found in 1680. It was cut into a brilliant and, after many adventures, came into the possession of Catherine the Great of Russia, who had it mounted in the sceptre of the Czars.

Another celebrated Indian diamond was the Koh-i-Noor (the mountain of light), discovered in 50 B.C. and remaining in the possession of Indian princes until in 1850 it was presented to Queen Victoria by an English lord who had conquered the Punjab. There is a legend that this stone will bring bad luck to England so long as it is not returned to the family of the Indian prince Vikramaditya. A noted Brazilian diamond is the Star of the South, weighing 260 carats, which was cut into a brilliant of 125 carats, and the *Southern Cross*, a rose-cut stone of 118 carats.

Other sources of diamonds are Borneo (now worked out), Surinam, the two Guyanas, Australia, North America and Russia. In the days of the East India Company, Borneo supplied many diamonds, among them the famous *Matan*, a very beautiful stone with healing properties in the possession of the sultan of Bantam (in 1787), who refused to sell it at any price to the governor of Batavia. Nevertheless, there were plenty of others, for Sir Stanford Raffles was to write later that very few European royal families could pride themselves on a collection of diamonds like those worn every day by the Dutch ladies in Batavia.

Another, notorious, stone is the *Hope* diamond, presented to Louis XIV by the French traveller Tavernier (born in 1605). Madame de Montespan begged to be allowed to wear it at a state ball and subsequently fell out of favour; Marie Antoinette wore it and lent it to the Princess de Lamballe; all three women were guillotined. After this, it came into the possession of an Amsterdam jeweller, who died destitute after his son had stolen it. The latter gave it to a gentleman called de Beaulieu and then committed suicide. De Beaulieu sold it in London to Eliason and died on the following day in strange circumstances. Eliason sold it to Hope for £18,000, and a member of the family, Francis Hope, sold it to an American, who got into financial difficulties and sold it to J. Colot, who committed suicide. The stone was sold to a Russian prince, who was murdered, and then came into the possession of a Greek, who perished in an accident after disposing of it to Abdul Hamid, sultan of Turkey, who nearly died shortly after losing his throne. A firm in New York bought the stone for somebody who was drowned when the Titanic went down; after this it was owned by a certain McLean, whose little boy was run over (1919).*

A diamond named the *Regent*, the size of a plum, was mounted on Napoleon's sword. It had been found by an Indian slave, who concealed it in a wound he had specially made in his body and tried to sell it through the intermediary of a sailor. The sailor, however, threw the unfortunate slave overboard and sold the diamond for £1000, made merry with his ill-gotten gains and then hanged himself. After this W. Pitt purchased the stone for £20,400 and slept each night in a different bed for fear of theft and murder before selling it to a French regent for £135,000. The stone disappeared during the French Revolution but came to light again and was mounted in the French imperial crown. Other notable diamonds are the Cullinan, the Excelsior, the President Vargas and the Florentine.

Jet

When we hear the word 'jet' we think of old-fashioned ladies in black dresses, the drabness of which is relieved by a plentiful sprinkling of bright jet choicely carved. This takes us back to the turn of the century or thereabouts. But then after the First World War, when women wanted to prolong their youth, the borders of old age were pushed back and the wearing of black dresses fell more and more into disuse. The year 1948 saw a renewed interest in jet, but by that time the old jet cutters were all dead and the demand could be satisfied only by what was found in jewel boxes inherited from old relatives. However, deep mourning was a thing of the past and if a black stone was sought for personal adornment the harder, more lustrous dark onyx was generally preferred. Jet is easily scratched.

Because it is so soft, jet can easily be worked and it has often been employed in jewellery ever since the Bronze Age. That it was popular in that period is evidenced by the armlets and anklets, the rings and necklaces found in the graves of that period. This is especially true of those areas in which jet was once mined: in Yorkshire and Dorset in England, in Schwäbisch Gmünd in Württemberg, Germany, in the South of France, Spain and in Utah in the USA.

Jet is highly compressed carbon thousands of years old. It is found in compact lumps and the surface of fracture has a resinous sheen. The

*It is now in the keeping of the Smithsonian Institution, Washington DC.

Translator's note.

material can be cut, ground and turned and was the basis of small industries in the places where it was found in former days, as for instance at Whitby in North Yorkshire and in Eskdale. In 1870 there were 1400 jet workers in Whitby alone making articles from both local and imported jet. Later on, imitation jet was manufactured from various materials such as glass, which is somewhat harder and heavier and is also colder to the touch. Genuine jet is a poor conductor of heat and feels warm. Rubbing it generates static electricity as in amber. When strongly heated in burns with a vile-smelling smoke, which used to be employed to treat the sick and in magical ceremonies. It need hardly be said that it is a stone of Saturn!

Jet is thought to be bituminous wood that has reached this state after being buried in mud. Fossilized wood occurs in the neighbourhood of jet, wood that has been wholly converted to pyrites or marcasite (iron disulphide) probably because it was softer and more porous than the timber we know today.

The jet used in jewellery has to be really black and opaque.

Pyrites
Pyrites or iron sulphide ore is found in blocks, in gravel or in crystals. Sulphur is extracted from it. It crystallizes in dodecahedra with pentagonal faces.

Nowadays, because of its golden lustre, it is mounted in rings. It has a powerful action and is given in homoeopathic doses as a remedy for inflammation of the air passages (a Moon-Mars affliction in Air Signs).

Usually it is called *marcasite* in the trade; also *Inca stone* because plates of polished pyrites have been found in old Inca graves. These plates have been taken for mirrors but may well have had a magical use.

Pyrites is more stable than marcasite. The stone is cut into small rosettes by machine for setting in jewellery. Inexperienced prospectors used to mistake it for gold on account of its golden gleam, hence the appellation 'Fool's gold'.

Marcasite
True marcasite also known as *white pyrites*, is lighter and more brittle than pyrites proper. It occurs as a shining crust on peat, clay and coal; also as crystals. When kept, it disintegrates in the course of time.

Dull on the outside but bright on the inside, marcasite symbolized to the old alchemists man in the fifth stage of his spiritual development in which, although he has been illuminated internally, he is still unable to communicate this illumination to the outside world. The phase in question is called the *marcasita*.

23.
STONES FROM THE VEGETABLE AND ANIMAL KINGDOMS

Amber	Bezoar
Pearl	Toadstone
Coral	Crab's eyes

Amber

Strictly speaking, amber is not a stone but the petrified resin of conifers which once grew in forests bordering the Baltic Sea. A natural disaster (that took place at the time when Atlantis was overwhelmed) caused these forests to be inundated, and the resin which had been exuded by damaged tree trunks was preserved under the water in the absence of air. Large pieces are now dredged up or washed ashore, one lump weighing as much as 20 lb. Some amber is completely clear, other specimens contain dead insects, fir-needles or splinters of wood. Cloudy stones must be exposed to the air for a while so that their essential oils can evaporate.

Amber is also found buried 90 to 120 feet deep in the tertiary rocks of Romania, on Sicily, in Burma and Spain and on San Domingo. This sort exhibits a blue-green fluorescence like petroleum.

Man has been using amber since the Stone Age. In the Orient it enters into articles intended for religious use, and Europeans have long been making mouthpieces for pipes, and beads, small boxes, bottles and other trinkets from it.

When amber is rubbed it becomes charged with negative electricity (as a matter of fact our word electricity comes from the Greek word *elektron* meaning amber). Amber is employed in both casting and breaking spells, for fumigating house and stable when they are thought to be bewitched, and also for hysteria, asthma, bronchitis (it warms the throat and windpipe), rheumatism, gastric catarrh, toothache, facial erysipelas, intestinal disorders, deafness, earache, poisoning, malaria, giddiness, pain in amputated limbs, bladder trouble and the evil eye. It is worn in necklaces for goitre, Basedow's disease and heart weakness. When reduced to a powder it was formerly taken internally. The reason for its use as mouthpieces for pipes is its disinfectant properties.

According to Greek myth, the tears wept by Phaethon's sisters after his death were turned to amber. Phaethon, the Sun god's son, had allowed himself to be diverted from the mid-path through the heavens when he was driving the chariot of the Sun and thus he met his death. The hidden moral here is that the man who squanders the creative force bestowed on him by the Sun in sexual pleasure will die spiritually, but those things in nature that are charged with solar power can still help the soul of man. And so amber makes a golden gift from the Sun even though it has lain at the bottom of the sea for thousands of years.

Although petrified animal products cannot be put on a level with stones from the mineral kingdom, we shall refer to one or two of them because their use and alleged working has so much in common with those of the genuine stones. In any case, why should they not possess notable properties, since they come as accompaniments to processes in the emotional life? Human gallstones form when people are suffering from repeated vexations as a product of Saturn-and-Mars activities, and human kidney stones come along with unhappy and disappointed love when there are conflicts between Venus and Saturn.

Pearl

The pearl arises in oysters and mussels, both of which are ruled by Cancer; and like human Cancer subjects, they clam up too tightly to be opened. A mussel on dry land keeps some seawater inside its shell, just as the human 'crab' clings to his or her personal emotional world. If a grain of sand or some other irritant is trapped in the animal, the epithelial cells on the outside of the soft body start secreting layers of a substance we call mother of pearl, and thus the pearl is formed within the shell. In 1554, someone suggested that pearls are the gallstones of the mollusc, but we should not be too ready to laugh at him. Others thought they might be eggs, while the poets fancied that they were raindrops that had fallen inside the open shell.

Not until 1904 was the riddle of pearl-formation solved. The particles around which Eastern pearls are formed are sometimes so small that they can not be found.

The *lustre* of the pearl is dependant on the temperature of the seawater, and its tint depends on the composition of the latter. Pink pearls come from Sri Lanka, cream specimens from the Persian Gulf; those from Burma are white tinted with rose, those from Japan are creamy white or greenish and those from Australia are greenish or bluish. Even brown or black pearls are found, and these come from the Gulf of Mexico.

If the pearl remains too long in the shell, it loses its perfect roundness. It is then known as a baroque pearl. The irregularity can be disguised by surrounding it with diamonds or some other gems in a piece of jewellery. Small natural pearls usually have a diameter of 8 to 11mm. From Burma come really enormous pearls of 16mm taken from very large oysters.

Before pearls were deliberately cultivated, pearl-fishers used to take their lives in their hands by diving for oysters in the depths of the sea, knowing that their lungs could burst or that they could be swallowed by a shark. In those days, pearls were very costly and, in wealthy families, ropes of pearls were handed down from mother to daughter or were given by a bridegroom to his bride as a wedding present. Often fresh pearls were purchased to add to the length of the original rope.

As early as the thirteenth century, the Chinese tried to make a pearl grow in an oyster by introducing fragments of mother-of-pearl or bone. The trouble was that the fragment stuck to the shell and had to be cut free. Present-day Japanese concentrate on cultivating pearls artificially; tourists can buy small tins containing seawater and a pearl oyster, or a small bag with a real cultured pearl. A tiny grain of mother of pearl 1mm smaller than the desired pearl itself, is placed in the oyster. The thicker the new layer is, the dearer the pearl. The cold Japanese sea gives the pearls more lustre, the warm Burmese waters allow them to grow to a larger size. Sometimes the nucleation does not take.

Pearls can last longer than men but are not immortal. They have been discovered in old Toltek and Aztek graves in Mexico, and in

Egyptian mummy cases. Some have even preserved a little of their lustre. Ear pendants and famous strings of pearls have survived from the Middle Ages, some specimens being set in gold. As a matter of fact, the Ancient Greeks used to hang pearl ear-drops in the pierced ears of their marble statues. Eventually, however, the fairest pearls become dull. Pearls like precious stones last longest when they are worn on the persons of healthy human beings. They need fresh air too. Some experts advise washing them in seawater from time to time.

Once they have been drilled and strung on gold wire, pearls make a delightful piece of jewellery, and some famous strings have been known to history. For instance, when the fourteen-year old Catherine de Medici was given in marriage to the French prince who was later to become Henry II of France, she was presented with a costly pearl necklace by her relative Pope Clement VII who, in addition, bore the expense of the wedding reception by pawning the largest diamond in his tiara. The necklace consisted of six strands and twenty-five tear-shaped pearls, the most beautiful anybody had ever seen. After an unhappy marriage, during which she was replaced in her husband's affections by his mistress, Diana de Poitiers, she was widowed when he was killed in a tournament. When her son, Francis, married the young Mary Stuart, Queen of Scots, in 1559, she gave her pearl necklace to the young bride, who was herself widowed at the age of eighteen when Francis died. As she sailed back to Scotland she clung to the rails of the ship gazing back at her beloved second home—'la douce France'—for as long as the coastline remained visible. Elizabeth I subsequently purchased the pearl necklace for £3000 from the Regent of Scotland, the 1st Earl of Murray. She loved collecting jewellery—in her own way. Through Antonio of Portugal the Portuguese pawned their crown jewels to her for English help, which was not forthcoming however. Elizabeth failed to return them. King Henry IV of France gave her the crown jewels of Navarre as security for 60,000 crowns for his army, but when his ambassador called to redeem them she suddenly demanded 300,000 crowns and finally retained the jewels themselves.

After Elizabeth's death, James I gave the pearl necklace to his daughter Elizabeth as a wedding gift, when she married the Elector palatine Frederick V, nicknamed the Winter King. After reigning for a single winter, Frederick was defeated and left his country in 1621 to settle with his wife in Holland, where they reared their thirteen children. Her daughter Sophie married the Elector of Hanover and when Queen Anne died without issue, Sophie's son George became king of England but resided in Germany as much as possible. His son, George II, let his fine-looking wife Caroline wear the famous pearls and they were shuffled backwards and forwards between England and Hanover in a royal jewel-case. They became known as the Hanoverian pearls. After George IV and his brother William IV had worn two royal crowns, those of England and Hanover, Victoria succeeded them. Since the people of Hanover were not in favour of having a woman on the throne, they made Ernst August, the last son of George III, their ruler and Victoria was only Queen of England. In 1834 Ernst August demanded possession of the Hanoverian jewels and as Victoria did not comply with his request but took the matter to law, a lengthy proceeding, he did not live to see the outcome. Hanover did obtain a pearl necklace but it does not seem to have been the one that had belonged to Catherine de Medici.

Pearls, then, seem to go hand in hand with greed, cruelty and female suffering. Has it not been said that pearls mean *tears*?

Coral

That splendid substance, coral, which takes the form of reefs growing on the floor of warm seas in Polynesia, off the coast of Japan and in the Mediterranean, is really the home built up by minute animals. Coral consists of calcium carbonate in the form of calcite mixed with some magnesium carbonate and organic matter. Black coral is horny. In the madrepores or stony coral each little creature lives in a white stony compartment that spreads out in ray-formations; in the millepores one can see individual pores and in the alcyonarian corals there is a great variety of colour and form, such as in the blue and pink organ pipe coral. The marvellous red blood coral or Corallium rubrum is the most frequently made into jewellery.

Ever since Roman times blood coral necklaces have been favourite costume accessories in Europe, to the extent of becoming traditional in places like Zeeland and the Gooi district of North Holland. The red coral was made into beads which were strung together in four strands fastened in front with a gold clasp. Formerly they adorned the necks of every farmer's daughter—now they are almost priceless. If the coral became pale, it was realized that the wearer was anaemic and very weak, for the beads were taking on themselves the early inroads of the anaemia and holding it at bay. Of course, red attracts the power of Mars.

Red coral also served as a protection against the evil eye, helped in cases of infertility and dealt with diseases induced by sorcery.

Bezoar

The famed bezoar stone was held in high esteem for many centuries as an *antidote to poison*. It was found in the stomach of Eastern goats, pigs and monkeys, which used to feed on all sorts of medicinal herbs that they found growing wild. Stones of this type consisted of a kernel or nucleus surrounded by successive layers of hardened material rather after the manner of a pearl. Great confidence was placed in the stones taken from the Persian Bezoar goat. Bezoar is derived from the Hebrew word *baalzazar*, and means master of poison.*

The bezoar stone used to be employed in many ways. A large piece would be dipped in wine by the apothecary and bottles of the resulting tincture would be sold to the patient for twenty-five florins. Other stones would be pounded in a mortar and administered in powder form. Another way of using the bezoar was to wear it as an amulet and a small one was often mounted in a ring. Pope Innocent XI (1676-89) collected many bezoar rings when he was still a cardinal. Louis XIV squandered money on them and used the stone for smallpox among other things. Bezoars were also tied over wounds to heal them.

Since these stones were mainly calcium carbonate, they worked to some extent like a cleansing salt and like charcoal, which sucks up injurious acids and poisons.

Toadstone

In Shakespeare's play *As You Like It*, we read:

> Sweet are the uses of adversity;
> Which, like the toad, ugly and venomous,
> Wears yet a precious jewel in his head.
> (Act I, scene 3)

This stone, called *crapaudina*, was sometimes white (and this was the best sort), sometimes brown; it had a small white patch like an eye in it. The stone is swallowed in a morsel of food and then absorbs all

---

*According to the OED, Random House and other dictionaries, bezoar comes from the Persian, *pad-zahr* and means counter-poison or antidote.

Translator's note.

poisonous substances on its way through the body. Albertus Magnus, the great magician, mentioned it as early as the thirteenth century, and Baptista Porta, writing in the sixteenth century, said: 'The stone Chelonites is found in the head of large old toads and is very curative if it can be taken from the living animal. The toad is placed on a red cloth for the colour pleases it very much. When it jumps, the stone falls out of its head and must then drop through a hole in the cloth into a box that has been set beneath it, otherwise the toad will quickly swallow the stone. There is not the slightest doubt about the value and operation of the stone, although I have never found one in spite of the many toads I have dissected.'

Now the toad is a very special animal, particularly the warty backed Surinam toad. It conducts the power of Pluto and therefore has to do with propagation and growth, for Pluto's power is that of embodiment in matter. Often one of the characters in fairy tales (e.g. that of Snow White*) is a toad who informs some lady that she is going to have a child. This piece of folklore is still current, and we recall someone telling us that when they were children she and her sister once saw two toads, a large and a small, and came to the conclusion that they were going to have a baby brother or sister. And so it came about: twins were born into the family, one child being bigger than the other.

When the power of growth is checked, it strikes inwards and causes warts, swellings, etc. On the principle that like cures like, people in Surinam bind a toad on cancerous tumours, claiming that this reduces the swelling. So it is not too hard to understand how in mediaeval times it was thought capable of antidoting poisons (if the sufferer could only find the stone in its head).

Crab's Eyes

So-called *crab's eyes* are not eyes at all, but stones mainly consisting of calcium carbonate formed in the stomach of the crayfish. An old writer tells us that, 'in the crayfish just beneath the head near the stomach grow two small pea-sized stones which are in the shape of flattened spheres hollowed out on one side and look rather like eyes. Nevertheless, this they are not since the creature has two perfectly good eyes in the usual place. In Latin they are called *Lapides cancri, Oculis cancri.*

---

*I cannot find the incident of the toad in the original Grimm brothers' German version of Snow White in *Kinder- und Hausmärchen*. But a frog foretells the birth of the 'Sleeping Beauty' in *Dornröschen*.   *Translator's note.*

They ease out teeth, dry weeping sores, neutralize acidity, are good for sweetening inveterate ulcers and blisters and for checking diarrhoea, bleeding and vomiting.'

What is more, the crayfish is also an animal of Pluto and is known as a remedy for cancer. There is a prescription in the old herbal of Brother Aloysius which involves pounding up living male crayfish with garlic in an earthen pot and binding the paste on a cancerous tumour. It has to stay there for twenty-four hours during which time the patient must be kept awake. After that the disease has entered the crayfish paste and the patient is cured. The writer quotes examples of this. Not by accident has a certain human type, that fails to rid itself of psychic poisons (and the Sign of the Zodiac to which it belongs), been given the name of the (closely related) animal and the disease: the Crab (often drawn more like a crayfish than a crab) and Cancer. The most striking characteristic of both is the collecting and retaining of unpleasant things.

So, who knows, there might well be some virtue in those crab's eyes.

As we have seen, *calcium carbonate* plays a prominent part in all these stones of animal origin. The general effect on the human frame is calming and purifying due to the trapping of poisonous substances. Calcium carbonate is employed in Homoeopathy and, according to the instructions of Dr Hahnemann, the founder of this system of medicine, it has to be prepared by triturating the middle layer of oyster shells. It corrects hyperacidity of the stomach (which expresses itself in a voracious appetite, thirst and a craving for eggs). It is helpful for persons of a scrofulous and neurasthenic type suffering from endless head colds and eczemas, mucous secretions and gall-stones.

INDEX